FAME
AT ANY COST

# FAME
## AT ANY COST

**KEELEY BOLGER**

**OMNIBUS PRESS**

London / New York / Paris / Sydney / Copenhagen / Berlin / Madrid / Tokyo

Cover designed by Fresh Lemon
Picture research Jacqui Black

ISBN: 978.184938.407.0
Order No: OP53460

**Exclusive Distributors**
Music Sales Limited,
14/15 Berners Street,
London, W1T 3LJ.

Music Sales Corporation,
257 Park Avenue South,
New York, NY 10010, USA.

Macmillan Distribution Services,
56 Parkwest Drive
Derrimut, Vic 3030,
Australia.

Typeset by Phoenix Photosetting, Chatham, Kent
Printed in the EU

A catalogue record for this book is available from the British Library.

Visit Omnibus Press on the web at www.omnibuspress.com

# Contents

# Acknowledgements

Thanks to everyone who has been interviewed for this book. Massive thanks are also due to Joe Minihane, Elaine, Ady, Shelley and Hannah Bolger, Ethan Ashbolt, the Arch family and the Minihane/Parkin family for all their love, encouragement and patience (especially with me banging on about this book for months).

# Introduction

"The winner takes it all, the loser standing small," sang ABBA in 1980. How little the Super Troupers knew. For just 20 years later the supposed 'losers' of reality TV shows would be cropping up and trouncing those who'd originally won the same competition they'd fought tooth and nail to win.

Winning might mean everything on a TV talent show but out in the world of the charts it means little more than the expectation that you'll dash out a Gary Wilmot cover and then fade faster than a polar bear in a blizzard. The only compensation is that people may remember that once upon a time you won a series of 'that show on the telly', you know the one with the judges and the drawn out elimination rounds, and they'll probably tell you that they expected you'd fail anyway. Cue a Nelson Muntz from *The Simpsons* 'ha ha' in your face. Lucky you.

It could go big for you, really big, but if it slips slightly then you're a failure. Nah. Winning is not where it's at. If you want a longer career in music, go for second or even better, third place. Without the pressure of expectations and cheesy first video to record, you'll be free to reap all the riches of winning and sing whatever you see fit.

But what is it about winning that bites the singer on the bottom once in the charts? Do runners up try harder? Do we inherently prefer underdogs? Let's take a look.

# Chapter 1

# *Popstars* – **Hear'Say**

There's a lot to be said for feckless grammar. The members of Hear'Say might have been too busy working on their silky tones at school to learn much about the correct use of apostrophes in the English language but their boo-boo won them an unlikely adversary in bestselling writer and punctuation authority Lynne Truss.

That greengrocer's apostrophe lumped between the Hear and Say of their band name was a sticking point for the *Eats, Shoots And Leaves* author who declared that the unsought apostrophe was "hanging there in eternal meaninglessness" and was a "significant milestone on the road to punctuation anarchy".

While the linguistic blip might have brought the world of punctuation marks out into the limelight – indeed rarely does a day go by without a shower of exclamation marks raining down over the internet and causing much tut-tutting aggravation – it's easy to forget that before this fresh-faced bunch found themselves in Ms Truss' bad books for not obeying grammatical laws, they were the bright young things whose stories and ascent to fame had us gripped.

Things started so promisingly for Hear'Say. Back in 2001, they were pipped for great things. All the ingredients were there; deftly handed a song that was co-written by the sublime Betty Boo (tick) and then songwriting and production team Jiant (tick); a throng of supporters gained from *Popstars,* the ITV show that gave birth to them (tick); chirpy band members who fizzled with excitement at being chosen for the group (tick); and the type of media coverage that most new bands would give their grans for (tick, tick, tick).

Whizz that all together and you'd be forgiven for thinking that a few years down the line Hear'Say would have plummy roles as judges on talent TV shows (reality TV circle completed), their expansive back catalogue covered by other pop stars, and be called upon to lend their faces and voices to benefit events for natural disasters organised by St. Bono and Archbishop Geldof.

Unfortunately, things didn't turn out that way at all for the newly famous five: Kym Marsh, Myleene Klass, Noel Sullivan, Danny Foster and Suzanne Shaw. But back at the start of *Popstars,* at the turn of the century, things looked a whole lot peachier. Back then, they weren't a band in the chart who took a maverick approach to the use of apostrophes, the bounders, back then they were just like us.

By virtue of this, those five boys and girls and their fellow aspiring singers showed the world that the seemingly impossible could be made possible; that pop stars who were really just people like us with jobs like ours, families like ours and high street clobber like ours, could be discovered and morphed into superdooperstars on a TV show.

They could be as unashamedly excited, as we might be, and scream down their clunky mobile phones (it was the turn of the century) to their mums, shrieking that they'd made it and weren't all those hours in front of the hallway mirror practising Bananarama routines worth it now, hasn't it borne fruit? And we could watch it all happen.

Tony Lundon was a member of the successful pop group Liberty X, formed of the five finalists who weren't chosen for Hear'Say. Tony reckons that although *Popstars* and the talent shows that followed it may be criticised for giving aspiring singers a platform to achieve their ambitions, or knocking them out through the rounds and broadcasting it, they are nevertheless important in fulfilling viewers' desires to see those dreams come true. Because, well, it is entertaining.

"*Popstars* was a fully pre-recorded, fly-on-the-wall factual entertainment series," says Tony. "Reality talent shows have evolved from *Popstars* into the Saturday night live TV mega-show you see currently.

"I enjoy *The X Factor*, but I have issues with it. There is too much airtime given over to contestants' sob stories, there is definitely something morally wrong about making fun, nationally, of the intellectually challenged, and it certainly feeds into young people's expectations of 'Fame, NOW'. But God, is it entertaining."

Tony's view of *The X Factor* making entertaining telly is shared by the 15m people who watch it week after week and the same can be said for *Popstars* back at the start of the Noughties. The format may have evolved but the genre is as popular as ever. It does make good telly and, handily, it also makes good business sense. It's the ultimate in music marketing: make a TV show about people who want to become singers, crown one – or one act – the winner, give them a song that will appeal to as many of that audience as possible, then bring out that single and watch it fly up the charts. Wham, bam, thank you ma'am.

There's also a better-than-evens chance that a good proportion of those viewers who watched the show and liked the singer's style will then go on to buy their music after they've won the contest, especially since – unlike subsequent TV talent shows – the five members of Hear'Say were chosen by judges 'Nasty' Nigel Lythgoe, Polydor A&R executive Paul Adam and head of promotions Nicki Chapman and not the public that didn't have a say in who they'd like in the band. It's a sort of modern day Monkees. Watch the show, buy into the band, support the band in the outside world, everyone's happy. In that sense, it's just a facet of the music industry and supplies a demand for accessible pop.

"Musos constantly criticise shows like this and pop in general," says Tony Lundon. "I see it like this: Hollywood makes blockbusters,

French auteurs make art-house flicks. There's completely different audiences for both. If you're like me, you'll go for a blockbuster when you want to be entertained, and an art-house flick when you want something more challenging. It depends on how you feel.

"Plenty of snobby musos will queue up with everyone else to see the latest blockbuster – a story that's been told a million times, but with new innovative packaging – but yet they have a problem when pop, the blockbuster of music, reaches a mainstream audience through mainstream media – an audience who want to be entertained. There's elements of snobbery, jealousy, stupidity and self-righteousness involved."

That there may be. But on the other hand, the throng of people who chose to switch on *Popstars* were entertained and probably wouldn't give two hoots about any bleating from the nay-sayers' camp. The drama and feats of striving singers giving it their all to win a place in a much-hyped band was entertaining enough for millions of people to keep watching it each week, and there was never any suggestion on the show that sooner or later it could all go kaput for the eventual winners.

At the time *Popstars* was a revelation. Ordinarily, pop stars are cautious about discussing their lives, and the magical process by which they became pop stars in the first place was a closely guarded secret. Depending on the audience at which they were targeted, the PR mechanism might reveal that they liked sitting in with their folks and watching *Corrie* and supping a nice cuppa or, at the other end of the spectrum, trashing a hotel room with a spanner because what else are they going to do with their spondoolies? This, of course, was the time before Twitter and 24/7 updates from stars about the delicious apple turnovers they'd just scoffed from Greggs the bakers.

Now, however, pop stars were made flesh and blood. In the past the only people who appeared on telly were those who'd already done things, important, horrible or successful things, and wasn't for ordinary folk like us unless we popped up as a talking head on the news about a neighbourhood dispute over a bushy tree partition or as an improbably excited contestant on the *Generation Game*. Now, anyone could get on these reality shows. Their blessing was that viewers knew everything about the wannabe singers and could form a connection with them via the airwaves.

We knew that Myleene Klass played the piano, violin and harp and therefore was definitely musically talented and definitely deserved a place in the band. We knew that Kym Marsh was the oldest of the lot – and later on that she had children – and therefore wasn't it good that the band wasn't simply made up of snotty-nosed A-level students, and weren't Labour always banging on about getting mothers back into work anyway? We knew that Danny Foster had worked as a cleaner and therefore had done his time toiling in an ordinary job – who would begrudge someone who'd earned his crust with a dustpan and brush?

Hear'Say were cut from the same cloth as us or at least the same as people we knew, and we were happy they were just like us and, in swearing allegiance to them on the telly, we somehow won ourselves, or at least shared in the win. We knew they were just like us because they were seen goofing up in front of big, important people, saying things that would make them cringe five minutes later. They were so real that they could have come from the same town as us. So we rooted for them and were glad that they were doing it for us ordinary folk, and weren't just a bunch of mewling stage-school kids looking to clutter the charts with their songs about fame.

Scores of viewers sat glued to the telly every Saturday night, hushing anyone who dared talk over any of Darius Danesh's soliloquies or dramatic finger points to the camera. Back then, it was a novelty to see The Dream of Becoming a Pop Star become reality TV. It was like an otherwise bog-standard caterpillar going about its business before entering the cocoon that was *Popstars,* and emerging as a fluttering, magnificent butterfly – and not just a cabbage white butterfly either, one of those painted lady varieties. It was music to our ears and even as reality TV further tightened its grip on our TV schedules, we could still find plenty of joy in watching that metamorphosis.

There was enough to keep us enthralled during the TV show and certainly when Myleene, Danny, Kym, Suzanne and Noel were finally told by the judges that, yes, get your tears of thankfulness and super-size Kleenex at the ready, they were the selected five, we might even have felt sorry for the other five contestants who went on to become Liberty X.

Hear'Say were worthy winners, and their joy was our joy, their excitement our excitement. In the absence of neighbours we knew or friends and family in easy reach, *Popstars* made community viewing, as has the rest of the talent TV show rabble that would follow in its wake.

Maybe it was a conscious decision by the judges but in the chosen five there was something for everybody, something for every pop fan. The caricatures were certainly appealing: the stunning Myleene Klass with her mane of swishy long dark hair (hello future shampoo adverts), ivory tinkling and love of classical music, the wild card if anyone claimed the band knew nothing about music; the smiley everyman Danny Foster who was down-to-earth, had a denim jacket for every occasion and had earlier tried his luck on Michael Barrymore's warbling game show *My Kind of Music* so we knew he Really Wanted It Really Badly; the feisty proud mum Kym – with a 'Y' – whom we rallied around when Nigel snidely huffed that "Christmas may be over but the goose is still fat" and whose straight-thinking personality and determination had us hooked; the bubbly Suzanne Shaw who'd already had small roles in BBC children's shows so we knew Loved Performing and that it was In Her Bones and was cut from a traditional-girl-next-door-who-joined-a pop-group cloth, thus fulfilling the cute quota needed for every pop ensemble of this ilk; and finally the cheery Welsh waiter Noel Sullivan who used to sing in a male voice choir – so had obviously Done His Time and Learnt The Ropes – who'd travelled the world and just wanted his shot at big-style fame.

Fraser McAlpine, who writes for BBC's Chart Blog, agreed it was the right blend: "I was initially pleased when those five members were the ones chosen for Hear'Say because I was vying for them all along and I was pleased when they made the band. I think the judges picked the right members for that group. Whether that was because the way it was edited so that we would feel they were the most deserving winners and feel satiated when they were chosen or because those five shone through I'm not sure, but I thought that they'd made the right choices for that band."

So far, so popular. And at the time they were chosen, we hadn't yet become saturated with reality TV pop. They were the first pop stars to be conceived on a TV show for yonks unless you count cabaret-trilling singer Jane McDonald who found fame on BBC's *The Cruise* and has now landed a cushy slot on ITV moan-along *Loose Women,* or the parent-friendly S Club 7 who were formed by *Popstars* creator Simon Fuller and given Enid Blyton-style lines to say to one another during their CBBC show ('Oh you muffin Bradley', 'You 'nana Hannah') and invaded the charts and silver screen thereafter. So it's no wonder that so many of us took to Hear'Say in the way we did.

With the release of their first single, 'Pure And Simple', Hear'Say further enhanced their command of pop. They had the dream combo of style and substance and the song eventually shifted a whopping 1,080,000 copies in the UK.

To put that in perspective, in late 2004 – a notably poor period for single sales – Eric Prydz's hands-in-the-air holiday anthem 'Call On Me', complete with video of hot babes working out in skimpy gym togs, sold just 23,519 copies, the lowest sales figure ever for a single that reached the top spot. The following week it slipped down but the week after that it was back at number one again, though Eric beat his own record by selling just 21,749 copies this time around. Conversely, the song was still the fourth biggest-selling single of that year.

'Pure And Simple' was originally recorded by Girl Thing who were tipped to become global superstars on the same level as the Spice Girls and for whom Simon Cowell toiled as their A&R man. They included the song on an international imprint of their album but did not release it as a single. So when *Popstars* judge Paul Adam heard the track, he thought it could be put to good use by the winners.

And – lo – it was put to good use. Hear'Say cosied into the number one slot for three weeks – and kept the already established Spice Girl Emma Bunton and Boombastic Shaggy busy trying to knock it off the top to make room for theirs. At the time, it was the fastest-selling debut single ever and one of the few singles in the Noughties to achieve double platinum status. Nowadays it stands as the ninth best-selling hit of the Noughties in a Top 10 that reads like a who's who of the decade's reality/talent TV spawn.

Also, the song matched the hype. 'Pure And Simple' won an Ivor Novello Award for the best-selling single of that year, the same award that had previously been awarded to pop greats like Kylie Minogue and The Bee Gees. For a band formed on TV, Hear'Say seemed invincible. At that moment, they made pop and their – or our, because we were with them, so it was sort of our success too – rise to fame look as Pure and Simple as the song's title.

But just because the band had had a golden goose on their hands in 'Pure And Simple' didn't mean that everyone connected with the song or with popular music went goo goo over it. Radio 1 DJ Chris Moyles moaned that it sounded too similar to Oasis' 'All Around The World', and recorded a parody that spliced the two songs together to prove his point to anyone who might have missed it.

The song's co-writer Betty Boo, who never met the group, was critical of the band's version of 'Pure And Simple' and of the way the group had found their fame. A *Smash Hits* era pop darling, Betty was wary of the way pop music was being handled, played out and placed in the hands of certain music industry executives who found their way onto the telly.

"*Popstars* was the whole thing I completely loathe in pop music," Alison Clarkson, aka Betty Boo, told *The Guardian*. "I don't like the idea of people being auditioned to be in a pop band. They may as well be working on a cruise liner. Pop music will not evolve if it carries on like this.

"I think *Popstars* exposed how a pop group is made. It should put an end to it completely. Even if 'Pure And Simple' was a successful record, I'm not that passionate about it. I'm more passionate that the programme itself might have changed people's view about pop."

Tellingly, Alison was among the first to realise that Hear'Say's pop dream might not be all it was cracked up to be. "After 'Pure And Simple', it would have been a natural thing to ask the people who wrote it to write them another one. The chances are it would be another massive hit. But they didn't contact us or anything.

"A lot of record-company executives have their own agenda. A lot of them have their own music publishing companies and they try and use writers signed to those companies, so that they'll get a slice of the pie. It's very crooked."

Whether or not there was anything awry in the way Hear'Say were dealt songs is a matter for those inolved. Certainly, while Betty Boo has no shortage of pop know-how, none of the band has mentioned any disquiet in the ranks over the wisdom of releasing another uptempo ditty about everything being just ticketyboo if you work together and love one another.

Indeed, five singers who've just landed their dream, dream job with icing on the top in the form of a number one hit probably aren't that likely to swim against the tide. They weren't that type of artist; they were formed on telly and even if that doesn't necessarily mean differences of opinion will be easily cast aside, they seemed complicit and happy about the songs they were given to record. Certainly, there were plenty of songs to be getting on with as just three weeks after releasing 'Pure And Simple', their first album, *Popstars*, came out and hit the number one spot in the UK charts. It achieved triple platinum status in the UK and would become the best-selling of all their albums.

But this is beside the point. Betty Boo is right; the releases after 'Pure And Simple' weren't as consistent in quality or as successful saleswise. They weren't as catchy. Then there was the inescapable fact that all this exposure, the inside-out X-ray knowledge we were fed about them and their collective and personal histories, the immediate success of 'Pure And Simple' and the subsequent press about its success and their reaction to its success, meant that we were getting bored of them by the time they released the follow-up three months later.

Nevertheless, the sappier, less hummable 'The Way To Your Love' still got to number one and stayed at the top spot for a week. But it had none of the bite of their first pop offering and in that respect seemed to be a taster of what was to come music-wise for the rest of their short career. By this point, of course, their celebrity had peaked and was now starting to wane.

In the event, the band had little time to mull over whether the second single was going to cut it with critics or whether it was the right choice for them artistically. There was no stopping the runaway Hear'Say train now the wheels were in motion.

Indeed, after the band pushed out their second number one single, they had to film the inventively titled ITV shows *Meet The Popstars* (as if we hadn't already met and seen their mugs often enough by now) and *Hear'Say: It's Saturday* (same again really). They were everywhere, ubiquitous, and they were cheesy. They sang Carpenters songs to each other on TV. Interest in them dipped. The suffocating blanket coverage was too overbearing and did nothing to help the band's cause. Hear'Say this. Hear'Say that. Bor-ing. Too late. Next please.

"Their problem was that after 'Pure And Simple' and to some extent before it, they were everywhere and their other songs didn't cut it," said Fraser McAlpine. "[They] had a brilliant first single in 'Pure And Simple' which was… a lot cooler than you'd expect for a song recorded for a reality TV-formed band but anything with Betty Boo's stamp on it is likely to be great because she understands great pop songs and she has a credible background.

"So understandably, it looked like things would work out for Hear'Say because at the point of bringing out 'Pure And Simple', even though they were over-exposed, they had a good musical product and so in some ways they lived up to the hype, because their debut single was good enough to deserve to be number one in the charts.

"The fact is that if you don't have the music to back up your publicity machine's claims that you are the most exciting, revolutionary pop group in the world, then people aren't going to keep spending their money on your singles and albums nor are they going to keep bothering with you.

"They were the most hyped band of the decade. But they didn't have good enough music to keep fans interested and people are always going to bring you down a few pegs if you don't deliver after all that hype.

"They might have supported you while you were on the TV show but it doesn't mean they have to follow your career if your career isn't that great. Their TV and music careers were two separate entities and while they were popular on the TV it didn't follow that they should be as popular in the charts.

"There's no shortage of pop acts around to cater for people's tastes and, in the case of Hear'Say, there were other bands doing what they set out to do but better and with less exposure."

While pop fans may have more patience when big stars like Madonna put out a duff single, they're not just going to politely look the other way when a new super-hyped band does the same thing, in the hope that they'll take note and bring out something more appealing next time.

"Only massive, established acts can get away with a few duffers and that's because they've already put the hard work in," said Fraser. "They've made consistently compelling music and are intriguing and interesting in a way that you can't be when you've revealed it all on TV and have come across like a nice, normal person.

"Pop stars need to have weird impulses that we don't understand. They need to say odd things and be compelling as well as make music that people like, believe in and fans believe deserve to be at the top of the charts. Just look at Lady Gaga. She says something interesting every day, wears something utterly bizarre, nurses odd hobbies and people love her. The blogs, the tabloids and people all over the world are interested in what she says, what mad hat she's wearing on her head and what she's up to. People haven't tired of her because her songs are great, her look is unusual and her attitude is different. That works in pop. Pop thrives on it.

"With Hear'Say, they were just everywhere after 'Pure And Simple', and that level of exposure didn't feel justified with the songs they brought out. The songs in themselves weren't bad as such but with the band being everywhere, people got bored of them and rebelled against it all.

"You can see why people would think they'd got above themselves because they'd gone from being plain Jane waitresses and cleaners with lofty ambitions of being singers to advertising any product going, lending their names to anything going, all within months of winning a place in the band."

Yet our gripe with the band came not with them personally – after all they were pretty decent eggs, not least Danny who was gainfully employed as a youth worker before entering *Popstars* – but with the manner in which they were marketed.

"The Hear'Say backlash wasn't about the members personally," confirms Fraser. "They were shown as nice people on *Popstars*. They were just five singers who wanted a chance to be pop stars. They didn't do anything wrong as such, they went into a TV show and were given the chance to become pop stars afterwards, but some of the music they were given didn't live up to the admittedly huge hype.

"That besides, the approach of their management to marketing and publicising the band was too overpowering. That might have been because they were the first band to come out of the reality TV canon and people were interested and so of course it will be on TV, radio, magazines but it was still too stifling.

"To top it off, we'd watched them for months on TV going through the process of becoming a band and then there they were again on every TV show going, every radio show going, every magazine going talking about the show and their experience of becoming a band and saying things we already knew, because they were in the papers and on the telly every day talking about the same things over and over again.

"Their songs were rushed out: two albums in a year, single after single without any proper thought as to what would work well for the band, what was popular at that time and what their fans would want to listen to. It was just a rush to get things out while people were still interested but it backfired."

Furthermore, Fraser reckons that there wasn't enough consideration for the type of music their fans would want to listen to. The result was a decision to go down the route of mushy tweenie pop rather than account for their original fans' maturing tastes. The UK and Hear'Say's original fans had largely turned a corner and moved on to the next new exciting band.

It just so happened that that band was Liberty, soon to become Liberty X*, the supposedly cast-off pop stars, the cruelly named 'flopstars' who didn't make the final grade to become Hear'Say but instead would whizz past them and go on to do bigger and brighter things. Indeed, in hindsight, it seems that Liberty X have had the type of career that Hear'Say were supposed to have: well-respected, longer, and with bit more dignity in their approach.

"Hear'Say's fans would have changed between the time they were on the telly and the time their first album was released," says Fraser. "They might have been 10/11 years old when they watched them on *Popstars* and might have wanted to listen to cutesy teeny-pop, but after their first album was released they probably changed their minds and thought them pretty uncool especially as the market for that type of music had faded.

"And what didn't help with that uncool was that you'd go into any Woolies in the country and their Hear'Say dolls would be there, stacked up and staring back at you. The five of them were on every advert in the land.

"They were on every TV and radio channel. People quickly got sick of seeing them especially when six months later, Liberty X formed out of the five finalists who didn't make the band, came out

---

*The X was added when *The Sun* ran a competition to come up with a new name for Liberty because there was a French act with the same name who took them to court although, of course, they had never heard of the French band.

and were much sharper, much more adept at being popstars. They looked great, they had something about them and quite importantly, they seemed to have shrugged off any reality TV connotations.

"They had a couple of songs in the charts and then they brought out 'Just A Little', which not only was a brilliant pop song that they seemed to enjoy performing and seemed like they had much more control over their direction – which made them stand out even more as the real deal compared with the plastic pop of Hear'Say – but it was aided by having such an iconic video with them all clad in leather and dancing around their canes.

"Hear'Say would never have been given a song like that because it was too much of a risk, it was too edgy and that's why it was even better when Liberty X came out with it. No-one expected it.

"Even their clothes and style were much more edgier and much more pop star worthy than Hear'Say. That video to 'Just A Little' was one of the best of that decade and certainly one of the most well-known. Liberty X put effort into what they did, they found a song that worked for them and really thought about what type of group they were and it showed.

"They seemed to care about making great music and being good pop stars. We didn't know absolutely everything about them and from what we were told, we were supposed to think that they were the failures of that show compared with Hear'Say, which was completely untrue. It made their success all the better."

It wasn't so much about liking the members of Hear'Say less than those of Liberty X but a desire on the part of fans to champion a band who'd been dismissed so quickly yet who had risen from the ashes of the TV show on which they were formed and become mightier than the winners. As much as we like a winner, we also like a runner-up who'll come back fighting. Such is our national spirit.

"The desire to be in a successful pop band, which we all had before we auditioned for *Popstars*, was what drove us together and forward," says Tony Lundon, formerly of Liberty X. "Egging the begrudgers' faces was not primarily 'the dream', but it certainly focused the mind knowing that failure, again, would be a bad smell and difficult to wash off. When Liberty X did get to number one with 'Just A Little', the culmination of all their effort and the early dismissal of their talents made the achievement that bit better for the band.

"It was certainly that little bit sweeter when we did hit number one, knowing that we had been labelled failures only a few short months before. We were aware that *Popstars* was an incredible launchpad, that we may never have an opportunity like it again, and that was, to an extent, incentive enough to make it work – use it or lose it really."

Use it they did. The tide had turned and flipped to Liberty X. Bereft of the backing of the public and media early on, they adopted a steely determination to prove doubters wrong and a compelling story – the underdogs – to take with them on their charge up the charts.

On the other side of the fence, the days – glory or otherwise – of Hear'Say's fame were numbered, if not already over. Conversely, their sparkling debut, 'Pure And Simple', made the crash even harder because more was expected of them. Where was the ice-cool pop that they'd first dished out? Nicki, Nigel et all on the judging panel had reassured us that these five nobodies turned somebodies were the finest undiscovered pop talents around and yet the evidence pointed to the contrary, and belief in them as a band who could actually go the distance stuttered to a halt.

While Liberty X were busy scurrying away perfecting their sound in Richard Branson's V2 studio, Hear'Say brought out another album, *Everybody*, just nine months after their debut. It sold one fifth of the number of copies that *Popstars* did and the reviews were luke-warm. Further evidence that faith in the band had evaporated occurred when they were booed at summer pop roadshows by the same fans that followed their climb to fame just a year before. Furthermore, criticism from the manufactured pop industry came in the form of boy band Five, hardly guardians of pop music's rich heritage themselves with songs about bad table manners and six-pack-toting member Abz who later released reggae-lite 'What You Got'.

The rot really set in when the group was accused of staging a terrifying run-in with a gunman as they were leaving a gig. Meanwhile, there were rumours of friction within the group and 'crisis talks' taking place. Finally, in January of 2002 founding member Kym Marsh, who had begun a relationship with *EastEnders* actor Jack Ryder, decided to call it quits, citing a change of family commitments as the reason.

Nevertheless, Hear'Say decided to plough on, drafting in a new member to the line-up. But even this had to be televised in a six-part series of auditions that featured the group umming and ahhing over an assortment of dancers and singers who clearly weren't put off by the shift in public and media goodwill towards the project. One of those who did his thang in front of the band was Johnny Shentall, Lisa Scott Lee of Steps' other half, previously of pop act Boom! that achieved a number 11 hit with 'Falling' and appeared on the *Smash Hits* tour, and whose nickname was Beefcake.

Hear'Say decided Johnny was 'the cream of the crop' out of the 3,000 wannabe singers they'd auditioned. They praised his 'fantastic voice' and were chuffed that he 'shared our sense of humour, which will help him fit in quickly'.

But the dwindling company of fans who still supported Hear'Say didn't warm to Beefcake's inclusion in the band, nor the manner in which he had been drafted in. There was a feeling that the open audition was rigged because Hear'Say were already familiar with the Doncaster singer who had performed as a back-up dancer for *Top Of The Pops* shows filmed in Manchester.

Even afterwards, when it was discovered that a job lot of the dancers and singers Hear'Say had met along the way were auditioned for a place in the band but didn't make it through to the first round, the bad taste still lingered around the group.

At the time, of course, Hear'Say and their management tried to put a brave face on things by suggesting that the change in line-up offered a chance to breathe new life into the band. Paul Adam, who'd played a part in choosing the original members of Hear'Say for *Popstars,* admitted in the press conference that followed the new recruit that, "although everybody has written Hear'Say off, I think unfairly, perhaps a new band member will act as a catalyst for new success".

With Johnny on board, Hear'Say wisely scrapped their UK arena tour to give him a chance to adjust to life in the band and concentrated instead on the radio station roadshows where they were routinely booed and jeered. In August 2002, they brought out 'Lovin Is Easy', their only song with Johnny, which was more sophisticated and edgier – hello crop tops and bedraggled hair – and more in line with 'Pure And Simple'. The video even featured Tiana Benjamin who'd go on to play tricksy Chelsea Fox in *EastEnders*. It reached number six but it was widely speculated in the press – although not backed up by Polydor – that Hear'Say's label wanted the song to make number five.

But this wasn't enough to recoup the band's popularity.

Fraser McAlpine: "If you are the type of group like Hear'Say, the much-hyped pop band, you need to have consistent hits because your time frame in the charts is probably pretty short and even if getting in the Top 10 sounds like a massive achievement to us, for a pop band with all that money invested in them, it wouldn't be seen as such."

Tony Lundon agrees that it is in everybody's – the act, the label, the fans – best interest to get the music into the shops as soon as possible. It is a wasted opportunity not to hone in on the interest while it's there, especially in the fickle, ever-changing world of 21st century pop music. "Strike while the iron is hot," says Tony. "If the label is dragging its heels on a release the act will be complaining. If the label is releasing too early, the act will be complaining."

Often forgotten amid the kerfuffle over releasing albums are the reputations of the producers and writers involved. While it's easy to assume that everyone concerned will want the fastest possible release while the band is flavour of the month, their professional reputations are also at stake if the finished product is sloppy.

"Yes, A&R can get it wrong, can get distracted and not work the act hard enough, and can take the easy option of whacking an album together senselessly, but their reputations would suffer also," says Lundon. "I would say it's a shared responsibility between the label and act to get the best product in the shortest time possible.

"It's definitely possible to make it work – when the act, their management, and A&R are on exactly the same page, when the right signals are being sent to the industry, and the act kills themselves to impress every single writer, producer, journalist, promoter, agent etc. – then there's prospects."

HMV spokesman Gennaro Castaldo concurs: "Music is a business and the fact is that singles aren't the big sellers or the things that drive the industry or music fans forward any more. It'd be nice to think that singles would become relevant again but at the moment they're not. They're there to sell the album, which, along with tours, is where the money is at. A label generally needs three good hits to make a popular pop album that fans will buy.

"If those singles aren't all top five – and this applies to pop acts more than any artists from other genres – then the label might understandably lose faith in the album and the act and stop plunging money and time in them."

"With a group like Hear'Say, their label had to maximise their selling potential and output while they could because the market for an act like theirs wasn't strong and interest in them waned pretty quickly. The label had to cut Hear'Say's apron strings because they couldn't have salvaged that act.

"The public had lost faith in them, they'd stopped making number one songs and they'd tried every possible avenue they could to rejuvenate the band's appeal but it didn't come back. In *Popstars*, Hear'Say had broken the third wall. But out in the outside world they were treading on the broken shells of the show's own making."

This is not to say that the individual band members can't be successful in their own rights – because they've proved quite the opposite – nor is it to diminish their achievements, but as a band and a brand they couldn't go on any longer. In October 2002, just a year and a half after bringing out their first single, Hear'Say announced they were splitting up, citing the public's indifference towards them as the reason.

In a press statement released after the group's split, Hear'Say's spokesperson stated that the band, "had lost the support of the public and Hear'Say had come to a natural end". (As another kick in the molars, 'comedy' bank NatWest made an advert wherein some buffoons in the bank were trying to work out what young people would least like. "A Hear'Say mousemat," one guffawed.)

It would perhaps have been easier to grit their teeth and announce with painted smiles on their faces that they wanted to focus on other commitments, start new projects, get on with that range of luminescent shoe laces they'd been wanting to design, while they were on a high – just like *Fawlty Towers* and *The Office*.

Instead they displayed the same honesty and unfailing sense of reality that could only come from the mouths of a band developed on a warts-and-all TV show. They weren't ending on a high. They wouldn't have *Newsround* issuing helpline numbers to parents worried that their offspring would take the split badly. They didn't have one last golden moment in the charts or in the public's affection. They were over because we'd moved on, and decided they were a cartoon-like joke.

"We have had enough. The public make you and break you," Danny Foster told *The Sun*. "Hear'Say was a phenomenon at the time and people have seen us grow and evolve into pop stars. We were just cleaners and waiters. It's been hard work and the pressure has got too much. Two months ago we were held up by a gunman and the next day people thought we had made it up as a publicity stunt."

Danny's fellow Hear'Say-er Suzanne Shaw was equally hardboiled about the reasoning behind the band's split, going as far as to note that the group and the way they were formed was just a trend, no less than the Nineties craze for wearing Global Hyper Colour T-shirts, which changed colour with a dip in temperature, or the subsequent fad for electronic Tamagotchi pets. "It's a fad thing, a novelty," Suzanne told *The Sun*. "It's like a pair of trainers, one minute they're in and the next minute they're out."

Their crime, so it seemed, was not so much to have been in and out of favour so quickly, but of being ordinary folk with ordinary jobs and ordinary lives who'd done well for themselves. "What they [people] didn't like is that we lifted the lid on the whole thing and people saw that you were just like Joe from down the road," said singer Kym Marsh to *The Sun* after leaving the band.

Hear'Say will always be remembered, if only for their almighty demise; the successes of 'Lovin Is Easy' and the range of plastic dolls pales when followed by such a monumental drop in popularity.

"Hear'Say will always be remembered as the first band to come up on TV and make a go of it in the charts afterwards," says Fraser McAlpine. "I don't think the way they ended would have put off any other aspirant pop stars because if you wanted it that badly, having what Hear'Say had and then being knocked down as soon as you'd reached a level of success would be better than nothing at all.

"They had a number one album and singles and for a short time were on top of the world. But I do think they show the way in which pop fans want more from pop music than just a catchy song. They don't really want to see someone just like them and their mates in a band.

"There's no aspiration in that. It's fun for a while but to succeed you need to have charisma and a performer personality as well as good songs. The TV show *Popstars* took that away from them because the most interesting thing about Hear'Say was that they were on a TV hunt for a new pop band. But then, we all knew about that because we watched it and didn't need to know any more about it. Besides, there was soon *Fame Academy* and *Pop Idol* after *Popstars* to fulfil those needs in the audience, so even the TV programme they were formed on began to look really outdated.

"People want more from pop. They want escapism as well as good tracks. They want to read about all the bizarre things their favourite pop stars have been up to, and Hear'Say by definition were never going to be able to achieve that because we were with them throughout *Popstars* to making it in the charts. What more was there to know about them?"

Evidently little that would recapture the initial interest. Besides this, Tony Lundon reckons that the level of control placed on Hear'Say muffled any decision-making within the band and the weight of expectation placed on them would have made it difficult to flourish. "I'm glad that I didn't get a place in Hear'Say on reflection because I got on better with the people I ended up in a band with," says Tony. "And if I'm honest, I liked their voices more. On top of that, I got to write and produce singles for Liberty X. That was my main contribution, and my main reason for wanting to be in a pop act in the first place.

"I am sure I would not have had the opportunity to do that had I been a member of Hear'Say. Why was it over quickly for them? Hear'Say were tied in to a certain deal and all the major decisions seemed to have been made for them, so how were they ever going to feel like they had any modicum of ownership?

"They probably endured a lot of pressure, and traditionally the first to leave a pop band – Robbie Williams, Ginger Spice, Brian McFaddon from Westlife – gets a solo deal. So Kym Marsh probably jumped the gun a bit early based on the fact that she had little allegiance to the other members or to the brand itself. And the A&R for the band wasn't great."

All these factors together make for an uncool concoction, especially when held up to Liberty X, says BBC Chart Blog writer Fraser McAlpine. "They didn't deserve the backlash they got but you can understand why people lost interest in them very quickly. No one thought to work on their music, it was just a big rush to keep getting songs out there and taking every deal while they could without any consideration for the public and the fact that very soon they'd tire of them."

So Hear'Say was over and original losers Liberty X became the winners. While Hear'Say had released four singles – three of which failed to recapture the cool pop slink of their debut, 'Pure And Simple' – Liberty X infused theirs with some hunky dory R&B and worked with of-the-moment producers like Richard X. Their original name, Liberty, was chosen because it stood for a sense of freedom from what they reportedly saw as the rigid structure in place for Hear'Say, and they now seemed detached from the TV show on which they had met.

Fuelled by a passion to make music together as a band and prove the disbelievers wrong, they worked hard on their material, their style and meshing as a group, and it paid off in spades. Even their record label – Richard Branson's V2 – had more kudos to it. "V2 took a chance on us, probably to an extent because Richard likes to be a patron to the underdog," says Tony Lundon. "V2 sent out the right messages to the industry, i.e. songwriters and producers, that we were a priority and that they would promote us properly. This led to writing and recording sessions with the right talent, and ultimately to finding the track to launch us, 'Just A Little'.

"Songwriters and producers need to know that their track has the best possible chance of success before they will risk giving it to you. Or sometimes they'll give you a track that has been turned down by everyone else, so they settle for a cut, any cut.

"I heard through the grapevine that 'Just A Little' was initially pitched to Anastasia – who turned it down. I also heard Jamelia's 'Superstar' was pitched to our A&R, who turned it down without ever mentioning it or playing it to me."

They may have missed out on 'Superstar', scooped up by Jamelia's people, but in 'Just A Little', Liberty X had a song that would elevate them from the ranks of acts who appeared on telly to proper pop stars who were not only great compared with other TV-formed bands but really, really great compared with other pop stars doing the rounds; a band for the nation to take to its bosom.

"I think for any band to have the best chance of success, all the angles need to be played successfully, at the right time," says Tony Lundon. "One of those angles was being on *Popstars. Popstars* gave us massive TV exposure. It linked viewers to us as individuals first, then as a pop band. Another was the way we were handled in the press. We were being labelled 'flopstars' and 'rejects', which helped to create an underdog impression, which in turn set the stage for people to get behind us when we found the right track.

"Being signed to V2 also helped, as did releasing the right track in 'Just A Little'. We, and by 'we' I mean the band and management, were also committed to maximising the opportunity and working hard to achieve success. That meant working, gigging, promoting, writing and recording incessantly. Say no once and that door you've closed never re-opens, so we had to be willing and I suppose we had to be able as well.

"Luckily enough we gelled well as people, our strengths as performers complemented each other, our weaknesses were masked somewhat by each other.

"V2 would probably not have been able to risk millions of pounds on us if we hadn't demonstrated the level of our commitment, which included writing and recording half an album at our own expense, before we were offered the deal.

"I guess some of our success also has to be attributed to luck. Why do some people, some songs, some videos capture the imagination of the record-buying public? You can prepare enough to take full advantage of an opportunity, but some added indefinable extra needs to kick in – luck. Some claim to be able to predict the zeitgeist's fluctuations in taste – bollocks. You can be keyed in for a time, and then time passes. No artist stays truly relevant to the chart."

James Fox was a contestant on the second series of *Fame Academy* and lived with Tony Lundon for a while. He thinks the band had more success than the winners, Hear'Say, because they had time to work on getting the best songs and working out the best route for them rather than just rush-releasing songs straight after coming out of *Popstars*. That aside, they didn't have the weight of expectation to get songs out so quickly and were afforded more time to perfect their sound.

"I think because Hear'Say were the first act to come out of one of these shows the pressure was really on for them to have a single out straight away and really grab the success while it was there," says James. "They didn't really have time to work on an image or a sound or find out what would work for them and see how best their voices blended and what sort of music they were suited to as a band, all of which might have helped them stay around a bit longer.

"It was just thrown together really quickly and they hadn't had any exposure to it beforehand. They were ordinary people who were put on TV and then made super famous and they could have had no preparation for that because no one would have known how much the programme would take off.

"But then a bit too late in their career, they realised that they hadn't quite got the branding or songs right for it to work for them as a band but by that point, it was too late to change it.

"People got sick of them because they were rammed down people's throats and so they didn't really have the opportunity to come back and do things differently because the goodwill for them had gone by that point. Even if they'd come back with a really strong song, I don't think they would have got people back on side.

"On the other hand, Liberty X worked on their sound and their voices with the producers and it turned out that that sound was cool and cutting edge. They had a great image, really cool and they had great songs and content. Plus they capitalised on being the underdog in *Popstars* but essentially what worked for them is that they had really great songs.

"Hear'Say should have gone away for a year like Liberty X. Liberty X did very well and I think they can be proud of all they achieved.

"It's always going to be a short life in pop anyway but they had a great run of it, earned money and had fun. I think Hear'Say just needed a little longer to work on their sound and what they wanted to do with the opportunity they'd been given but at that time, no one had been on a programme like *Popstars* so no one really knew then what would be for the best."

Despite Liberty X's credibility and success – they accepted a Best British Single Award from Bee Gee Robin Gibb at the 2003 Brit Awards for 'Just A Little' – Tony admits that the band were still viewed rather sceptically by the public.

"Many people, mainly those who enjoyed the show, were supportive of us. I wouldn't have considered them fans though. There was an inkling of what is now staple behaviour for *Big Brother* eviction night audiences, of jeering for its own sake, at some gigs."

And Tony, who says that while he enjoyed writing and singing in the band would rather concentrate on writing music and singing for fun, concedes that snootiness didn't come from acts who would be unlikely to be associated with *Popstars*, but instead from fellow chart stars.

"Muso snobbery certainly existed," he says, "but funnily enough, the snobbery that most affected me was when a moderately successful boy band, who shall remain nameless, threw a wobbler about being in a group photograph with us. We met many real music legends, like Echo & The Bunnymen's Ian McCulloch and Liam Gallagher, who displayed nothing but good grace.

"The music press and the media at large were initially and understandably sceptical, but I think at a certain point we achieved enough to change many people's minds. MTV was probably too self-consciously 'cool' to ever backtrack, so they constantly had us as guests on their shows but didn't playlist our videos."

Tony remains positive about his time on *Popstars* and during his hugely successful career in Liberty X and attributes much of this to going on the ITV show in the first place. "If I could turn back the clock I would still do *Popstars*, but if Liberty X hadn't have worked out, I don't think I would have applied for *The X Factor, Pop Idol* or *Fame Academy*. *Popstars* definitely helped my career in entertainment and I have no regrets about going on the show.

"In fact I'm grateful to have had the opportunity. That being said, I would probably have made more money if I had gone to college. You line the pockets of many people along the way, and often end up wondering how the system got to be structured the way it is.

"Of course there are things that could have been done differently, but for the most part I don't care if some of the videos, vocals or songs make me cringe in the future, or how much my mates take the piss out of the clothes I once wore – for one perfect moment, we got it absolutely right, we got to number one in the charts and fuck the begrudgers!"

Tony hopes to write more music in the future but at the moment doesn't want to be in the limelight. Likewise, the other members of Liberty X seemed to have gone on to other things after their time in the popular band. Kevin Simm from Chorley, who appeared on Channel 4 celebrity sports show *The Games*, has released his own solo album, *Brand New*, on iTunes.

His female bandmates Derby-born Kelli Young and Lancashire lass Jessica Taylor formed a dance act Danger Minx. Jessica, who is married to cricketer Kevin Pietersen, returned to ITV to compete in *Dancing On Ice*. Gateshead gal Michelle Heaton appeared to be popular with the public when she appeared on *Celebrity Big Brother* 2009. Liberty X seem to be fondly remembered, seemingly better supported once they'd split than Hear'Say.

On leaving Hear'Say, Myleene Klass went back to her classical roots and achieved considerable success with the two albums she released, even getting a nomination for the People's Album of the Year at the Classical Brit Awards. Things improved further in 2006 when she appeared as a contestant in *I'm A Celebrity… Get Me Out Of Here* wearing that skimpy white bikini and eating kangaroo testicles on air. So that's how you do it.

Out of all the ex-Hear'Say members, Myleene seemed to have been dealt the hardest hand. Rumours that she and Kym Marsh were at odds with each other didn't do much to help her appeal. "When the band broke up I was called ugly, untalented, unemployable and I was still in my early twenties," Myleene told the *Daily Mail* in 2009.

"I was on my own and so isolated. I was stuck in my flat a lot of the time. My mum would try to drag me out but I couldn't bear it. I thought everyone was staring at me. It sounds a bit indulgent now, but I guess at the time your problems are heightened because everyone knows them. I'd gone from playing in front of thousands at Wembley, my platinum discs were on the wall, but now I couldn't get arrested. I thought my life was over. I wouldn't say I was actually depressed but I was hugely gutted.

"All these people who say they can't cope with being famous are lying because it is a little slice of heaven really. I lost my voice when Hear'Say finished – I was so unconfident. Everyone seemed to hate me and I couldn't speak up."

It might have taken a long time for things to turn around for Myleene but fortunately bad feeling towards her seems to have diminished now. It's gone quite the other way and whereas before she might have been sneered at, she is now everyone's favourite TV big sister, smiling her way through several top-notch presenting contracts and putting a sisterly arm around any sobbing pre-surgery ladies on *10 Years Younger*.

Being the first one out of Hear'Say, Kym Marsh did go on to have a solo pop deal. Two Top 10 singles – 'Cry' and 'Come On Over' – followed but after the third – 'Sentimental' – went to number 35, Kym was dropped. She also tried that well-trodden route of applying to represent the UK in the Eurovision Song Contest but lost out to cruddy rapper Daz Sampson. But a return to fame came in the unlikely form of ITV soap *Coronation Street* where Kym has played the feisty firebrand – and fan favourite – Michelle Connor.

Similarly, Kym and Myleene's bandmate Suzanne Shaw has just been given a new lease of life in the shape of fellow ITV soap *Emmerdale*. Suzanne's name was kept in the press due to her relationship with tabloid 'love rat' Darren Day and appearing in *Dancing On Ice* (which has become a sort of retirement home for former ITV reality TV contestants).

Noel Sullivan, who popped up in an episode of *Gavin And Stacey*, has worked on several musical productions including *Grease*, *Fame* and *Loveshack,* while Danny Foster is still touring the country, working as a soul singer.

It seems to have taken a long time for the band to shake off the Hear'Say albatross around their necks but the five original members have gone to on better things, no small achievement in view of the condemnation heaped upon them. "For the type of music Hear'Say were recording and performing, they came out at a really bad time," says Gennaro Castaldo. "That type of ultra-manufactured pop had gone out of fashion and people didn't buy into it.

"It's not the band's fault nor was it the fault of their label; music tastes change so quickly and no one can really predict what will be popular but it just didn't work for them, and the longer they hung around performing songs that were seen as unfashionable the worse it got for them. People thought they'd outstayed their welcome.

"They were the first band to come out of a reality TV show, so what's good about that in a way is that they will always be remembered whereas a lot of people go on TV and are never heard of again. However, what is a shame for them was that there was no knowledge of how things would pan out afterwards.

"With *The X Factor* now and even *Pop Idol* and *Fame Academy*, there's some sort of inkling of the types of careers people go on to have afterwards, even if it is only a small inkling."

They could have done worse; they could have been One True Voice from *Popstars: The Rivals*. "I feel that Hear'Say have done a lot better than other winners. One True Voice for instance," says *Pop Idol* contestant Aaron Bayley.

Now, talking of One True Voice...

# Chapter 2

# *Popstars: The Rivals*

So to the perfectly formed pop princesses, Girls Aloud. Formed on ITV's *Popstars: The Rivals,* the five girls were – *quelle horreur* – seen as the poor relations compared with One True Voice, the boy band formed on the programme with whom they were supposed to compete in the Christmas singles charts.

The show, a sort of branch of the *Popstars* family tree, set itself up to find two groups – a boy and a girl group – out of thousands of hopefuls and then launch them at the same time, Christmas singles week – ooh the tension! – and have a different judge looking after each band to ramp up the drama.

With Davina McCall at the presenting helm and raspy Geri Halliwell on the judging panel, girl power was in abundance. But even so, everyone expected that the girl group would fall flat on their faces when it came down to getting out 'there' and releasing their single. After all, weren't Westlife the omnipresent pop stars of the day? How could any girl group compete? How little we knew.

"People were writing off Girls Aloud throughout *Popstars: The Rivals*," says BBC Chart Blog writer Fraser McAlpine. "Everyone expected that One True Voice would do much better than them in the charts because it was the year of Westlife and it just felt like it'd be a foregone conclusion that they would be the ones with the long-term careers."

When the five girls of Girls Aloud won, they took a different tack to the boys in releasing a much cooler-sounding pop song. In escaping the usual drivel dished up to winners Fraser thinks they helped give their careers a fighting chance.

On the flipside, Pete Waterman's group One True Voice – or OTV as they were never known – trod down the well-worn path of The Winners' Ballad. Theirs was a double A-side 'Sacred Trust'/'After You've Gone'. It reached number two behind Girls Aloud's 'Sound Of The Underground', which was described by *Guardian* music critic Alexis Petridis as "a reality pop record that didn't make you want to do physical harm to everyone involved in its manufacture". Phew.

"Girls Aloud decided that they weren't going to do so well peddling to the pattern of the show's previous winners and instead went off and did their own thing," says Fraser. "They got producers in who worked on a sound that was interesting and they came up with amazing pop songs. They looked good and have opinions about things.

"They worked with people who'd never heard of them before and, in turn, gained fans in people who'd never watched the show. People who bought their songs and became fans of their music did so because their music is great. They started off well with 'Sound Of The Underground', which was way cooler than anything a TV contestant has ever brought out before and it's no surprise that they are still around today and have done so well.

"They broke the mould – ballads! – in order to win the race between them and One True Voice, and by the time they did, no one cared that they came from a talent show."

While Girls Aloud were busy being all shades of marvellous, One True Voice, who have the dubious honour of being number 32 in *Chantelle's [Houghton] Top 50 Reality TV Stars*, brought out a second single, 'Shakespeare's Way With Words' (or Christopher Marlowe's depending on which side of the literary fence you're standing), which got to number ten in the charts in June 2003.

A few weeks later, member Daniel Pearce handed in his notice, saying he wanted to work on solo material. The very next day, the rest of the band made like a banana and split.

"In the case of One True Voice, it was a terrible name to start with but their split was mostly down to the worst A&R imaginable," says Tony Lundon formerly of Liberty X. "I have no doubt that those singles were forced on those lads – who were talented – by A&R decision makers who were so out of the touch, it astounded me."

Meanwhile, what of Girls Aloud then? What became of those five women when their rival band ceased to be? Well, they took over the charts and went on to blossom into the country's favourite pop band. "Part of Girls Aloud's success comes down to the fact that it was the right band at the right time," says HMV's Gennaro Castaldo.

"The UK needed a girl group we could be proud of. The Spice Girls had split up, the Sugababes were too busy changing their line-up, so there was a space in the charts and we needed a smart girl group to fill it. But the main reason they've done so well is that their debut single was incredibly credible and catchy and since then they've consistently brought out brilliant songs written for them by a team of excellent producers and writers.

"Their PRs were very clever early on to get them in the newspapers and tabloids, got us caring about who they were going out with and what they were wearing and what they thought about various things and, in a way, played to their celebrity appeal. They look great, they are great, they have brilliant songs. They deserve all the success they've had."

Tony Lundon thinks that Girls Aloud had fantastic material to work with from the off. "Girls Aloud had good A&R," he says. "From their very first single, 'Sound Of The Underground', the A&R was on the money. Either the girls are picking good tracks themselves, or more likely they trust the A&R enough to go along with the decisions made for them. Or, they don't have a choice, or they're a big happy family and pull together."

Q editor Paul Rees thinks that while Girls Aloud have had a great big dollop of success, the TV show they were formed on and the shows that have been spawned from it will never find the type of extraordinary acts who change music.

"These TV programmes have vast audiences so they really have no need to worry about appealing to self-appointed taste-makers. That would include me," he says.

"There are a couple of exceptions to every rule. And while Girls Aloud are an entertaining pop confection, no artist of substance or one that challenges the norm has emerged through these sausage factories. But that's not what they're for or who they cater for."

Whatever the music critics might think, eight years on Girls Aloud still pride themselves on their crusading pop, which hits the spot time after time. Their achievements speak for themselves really; Brit Awards, ITV specials, cameos in Brit-flicks, greatest hits albums, make-up ranges, judging spots on massive TV programmes, climbs up Kilimanjaro and fans in Noel Gallagher, Chris Martin and the Jonas Brothers. Much like their last single to be released from their fifth album, 'Out Of Control', they are pretty much Untouchable.

# Chapter 3

# *Fame Academy* **Series One**

When the BBC got a whiff of the whole talent TV trend, the corporation jumped on the bandwagon and put its own spin on the format. Sort of.

Not for the BBC the strung-out audition process and the swarms of great unwashed coming along to start a ruck if some jumped-up judge deemed their version of 'Chasing Cars' to be 'abysmal'. They did all that behind closed doors to save the judges' blushes and our ears the torture – and entertainment – of hearing out-of-tune cater-wauling.

Not for them the warbling along to well-known songs to get to the next stage of the competition. No, contestants had to do more than that or at least *say* they'd do much more than that. Learning when to artfully squeeze their eyes shut and when to clasp their hands to their chests during a rendition of 'I Will Always Love You' wouldn't cut it for this TV search for a star.

Neither would learning all the moves to 'Chain Reaction' and singing at the same time. Bubbly pop throng Steps could do that. They'd have to do something extra special to win approval and the TV-given right to become pop stars.

So welcome then the BBC's *Fame Academy* – which believe it or not also came with a panel of pernickety judges, excitable hosts and featured a live showdown each week not unlike say, *Pop Idol, Popstars* and *Popstars: The Rivals* — where they extolled the virtues of equipping the self-styled 'students' with the skills to go on to have a fruitful musical career. Inform, educate and entertain and all.

As such they were keen to let all and sundry know that just finely tuning some covers of ballads wouldn't cut it (well at least not until the second series when it was hello drama and big ballads, bye-bye boring old harmonicas), and that to stay perched firmly on top of pop's greasy ladder you had to have a bag-load of skills like composing as well as singing songs as well as positioning yourself in the market place and staying there. Look at Madonna. Look at George Michael. Look at Elton John. They all have those skills.

Handily, they made the programme into a reality format too, thus killing two passing TV trend birds with one big *Fame Academy*-shaped stone. Adopting the format of reality TV programmes and their requirement to catch unexpected, occasionally embarrassing, human behaviour, the *Academy* students were asked not to leave the mansion but to remain confined within its plush walls 24/7, keeping the big, bad world carefully locked out of their hermetically sealed all-singing, all-dancing planet. The best way to breed creativity is to lock up creative people with like-minded creative people, right? McCartney, Jagger, take note.

Unfortunately the contestants, though glad of the tuition they did receive, were generally expecting more guidance, more late nights chatting about writing techniques and semiquavers, and more direction than they actually received, and less of the performing up to the cameras trumpery.

Series two contestant Nick Hall said that the endless surveillance in the house meant that any potential creative spells were negated by its off-putting omnipresence. As such, the *Academy* wasn't conducive to making music, sweet music. If anything, the only creativity the constant examining of the students brought about was how to find different ways of twiddling thumbs in front of the cameras.

A crash course in media training it might have inadvertently been but although it is important for established stars to know how to handle the cameras and how to make themselves sound oh-so-salt-of-the-earth lest any fans go off them, the students didn't sign up for lessons in how to show their best side to the lens. *Fame Academy* was supposed to be more about teaching eager musicians about mapping out a career in music rather than teaching them about show-business.

"*Fame Academy* does little to give you any idea of the inner workings of the record industry," says Nick. "Being locked up in a *Big Brother* style house with less then 30 minutes of music therapy a day isn't really an academy is it? Most of the time was spent sitting around trying to think of things to do while the cameras watched us. Those that were better at this than others tended to last longer in the house."

Besides this, Nick also reckons that the offer to help new singers and songwriters polish their musical skills, and the constant assertions that *Fame Academy* was oh-so-different and oh-so-concerned about cultivating talent, was a pretence, that the show was nothing more than a televised karaoke contest, offering little of the help that a new singer-songwriter might need. This would have been fine if they'd said that from the off, but they didn't, maintaining instead that the show would be devoted to finding and nurturing music talent.

And despite many contestants' prior knowledge of the music industry, some like Nick had entered *Fame Academy* hoping to be told a trick or two about it so, armed with their superior knowledge, they could swan off into the sunset and make good headway in their singing careers.

"Prior to *Fame Academy* I'd been following a pretty successful career path in automotive engineering," says Nick. "It was something I'd done since leaving school so *Fame Academy* was a big change in my life. I'd watched *Fame Academy* series one and thought it looked like a 'better' idea than *Pop Idol* at the time as the premise was to take musicians/songwriters/singers and help them grow through a televised 'academy' type setting.

"*Fame Academy* series one turned out to be little more than *Big*

*Brother* crossed with *Pop Idol*, so I was not overly enthused by it as a TV programme. However, when *Fame Academy* two came along it had a bit more buzz about it being 'all about songwriting'. I entered the show with no preconceived ideas about how it worked and without really having a clue about the music industry.

"Contrary to popular belief, not everyone who gets on these shows has been 'chasing' the elusive record contract. I for one had only played music as a hobby, and had only been singing for a few years before the show.

"Throughout the audition process we all heard talk about potential masterclasses from George Michael, Sting, Pink etc and that Gary Kemp may be the headmaster figure. It all sounded like it would be 'more' than just a karaoke *Big Brother*. It turned out to be a big fat karaoke *Big Brother* after all."

If series two contestants were befuddled about the show's actual purpose and its long-term usefulness to them, series one's hopefuls were even more at sea. The programme advertised itself as a search for the UK's best undiscovered singer-songwriters. Yet the programme built itself on a reality TV structure that some students weren't aware of until they saw the many cameras planted in the house, which were shoved in their faces or followed them around the room, watching their every move.

"I had been playing in bands for seven or eight years in Glasgow and Edinburgh and not really getting a break when *Fame Academy* came along," series one winner David Sneddon told the BBC in 2005. "It was advertised for singer-songwriters. One of the better stories about it was that Nigel (fellow contestant Nigel Wilson) and I didn't know it was a reality TV show until we were actually on it."

Even though some of the contestants were unsure about the show's format until they were actually singing on it each week, they had plenty to be getting on with to distract themselves from pondering about reality TV too much. Once accepted in *Fame Academy*, contestants were packed off and kept as boarders at the plush London mansion (much like the rather magazine-spread-worthy digs offered to wannabe warblers in both *Pop Idol* and *The X Factor* and for added pop points, behind Sting's house) where the pop regime was drilled into them. They woke up each morning to have lessons in singing, songwriting and few dance classes thrown in for good measure and to give producers material to justify keeping the tapes rolling 24/7. These lessons were more in line with what the *Academy* advertised itself as: a training ground for musical talent. The hope was that someone hung up on the notion of being a big pop star would do something outrageously dramatic enough on camera to justify their existence and provide enough mettle for the main show and its two spin-off programmes.

Acoustic guitars and pianos were strewn around the *Fame Academy* HQ in Highgate as if to drum home the point that this wasn't like *Pop Idol*; at *Fame Academy* HQ we're all about real music and not just singing cover versions because that doesn't require real talent and won't cut it in the long run. The guitars seemed to be there to make the point that even though the contestants looked a bit similar to contestants on other reality TV or talent programmes, they were different because they actually played music.

While they were in the tutorage of the *Fame Academy* finishing school, the students from the first series were given an extra treat: lectures by respected songwriters, voice coaches and famous professors like Lionel Richie (who later popped up on the *Fame Academy* album with a song he'd written), Shania Twain, Ronan Keating and Mariah Carey, who between them had been around the pop block a few times and would be able to offer good, honest advice, and autograph their albums and T-shirts into the bargain.

This fixation on working on crafting musicians' talents rather than just, well, ahem, crafting their singing talent à la *Popstars* and *Pop Idol* was *Fame Academy's* unique selling point – until, that is, the producers realised that *Pop Idol* was more popular with viewers and the focus was thus shifted onto judges' comments and live performances.

This move may have pulled in more drama in the second year but the emphasis shift didn't go down so well with series two contestant Gary Phelan, who felt the change in direction gave the finalists less value for money. They were hankering for a bit more supervision with their songwriting and not just the chance to belt out a few Robbie Williams songs, which they could have just done down the pub. And frankly while they were in the pub, they could have had a nice pint, a game of cards and a packet of crisps too.

"To be honest I had hoped that *Fame Academy* would have been more about songwriting and playing instruments because that's what I'm good at and that's what I'm interested in," says Gary. "I thought that *Fame Academy* would have been more useful to me than it was. I think Sting put it right when he said a while ago that *The X Factor* is just glorified karaoke.

"But when you look back on *Fame Academy*, it's the same. The people at the end of the show got support for writing songs but for the rest of the show, it was more about singing covers week after week."

Back in series one though, the nerve centre of the show was the dream of becoming a 'real musician' and transforming the 12 contestants into 'real musicians' who, educated in the ways of professional songwriting, wouldn't be satisfied with having well-crafted pop songs dished out for them by an established writer at a record label when they could write songs themselves (and probably make more money for doing so).

The Academy would give its students upgraded pop credentials so they would be able to 'make it' once the cameras were turned off and host Cat Deeley had gone home. There was drama, yes, and indeed 'headmaster' Richard Park certainly ruffled feathers with his snide comments and criticism of contestants – which were turned up to 11 in series two – but series one set out to be much more about The Music.

Indeed *Fame Academy* even had a credible long-term vision to help and inspire more talented wannabes towards the path to musical success. Money from phone votes would go towards a Fame Academy Bursary to help people pursue their careers in music. (Interestingly enough, the Bursary is still going despite the programme being taken off the air in 2003, apart from the Comic Relief shows.)

David Sneddon seemed an apt contestant for series one. The eventual first *Fame Academy* winner, he not surprisingly loved music and wanted to hit the big time as a singer who could also take his musical ideas and convert them into his own songs. Thus far he'd not been given a chance to shine and wanted a shot at making it in the music industry.

*Fame Academy* presented that opportunity so David went for it. A budding musician from Paisley who'd played the piano from a young age and who had performed with his former band, The Martians, at the Edinburgh Festival, David had plenty of music credentials and a natural aptitude for the art when he applied for the new BBC search for talent in 2002. At the outset David seemed ideal to promote the *Fame Academy* party line that unlike the other shows this was the music show for proper musicians to launch themselves in a good and proper way.

As it happened, singer-songwiters were the coming thing. James Blunt had yet to leave the army, pick up his guitar and start singing about pretty ladies meeting unsuitable men at train stations and Damien Rice was still unrecognised and playing small venues, so the vacancy for a homegrown acoustic talent needed to be filled. Why not fill it with someone 'homegrown' via the telly?

In the event, David Sneddon wasn't initially chosen for the final 12, missing out on the public's vote when they were asked to call in and decide who they'd like as the twelfth contestant out of a choice of three wannabes, but when original finalist Naomi Roper dropped out of the show because of illness, David was swiftly drafted in and added to the roster of students in series one.

Once he joined the ranks David lost no time in impressing the judges and the public with his love of songwriting and his reverence for Elton John, further reminding everybody of his genuine desire to pursue music and that the programme makers had made the right choice in picking a real music fanatic.

"The person who has inspired me the most is Elton John," David later said in an interview. "I love The Beatles, but as I was growing up, I always wanted to play the piano like him. I've never had any lessons, so he has been my only teacher."

Certainly this cards-on-the-table admiration for Sir Elton was a refreshing change from, "I want to walk down the road and have people know my name. Oh and also, I'd very much like to be as big as Whitney Houston. No, actually bigger than Houston. That will do me." It put him in the bracket of Serious Musician Who Knows More than Just the Words to a Few Ballads.

Even if his impressive attestations didn't tickle viewers' fancies, David won over voters with his arms-in-the-air performance of 'Don't Let The Sun Go Down On Me' as well as his own composition 'Stop Living The Lie', which he was shown grafting over through the duration of the series. Art in action was the name of the game, giving viewers and potential record buyers the chance to get to know and like the song and then part with their cash once it was released, guaranteeing a wedge of success and hopefully a generous helping of radio and TV airplay.

As launchpads go, singing a self-penned song on a prime-time BBC light entertainment programme probably wasn't a bad kickoff to David's career in pop. Still, however much merit can be attached to David's likability and talent, much of the success of his single can be attributed to him being a TV winner.

Although *Fame Academy* was interested in the contestants nurturing their songwriting aptitude, series one songwriting mentor Pam Sheyne thinks that, without underestimating the contestants' achievement, the TV exposure certainly nudges potential music fans in the right direction – a skip all the way to the nearest music shop with a fiver at the ready to buy the single – for any talent TV winner, be it *The X Factor, Fame Academy* or any other ones floating around our TV waves.

Often, this is done with a cover of a well-loved song that can be quickly released to capture the interest while it's there, but with *Fame Academy,* it meant that David's self-scribed number was getting the exposure instead.

"Choosing songs for TV talent show winners is more political than just saying the art of songwriting is sacrificed for a quick release," says Pam. "The decision makers have their 'teams' they go to and understandably don't have the time to wade through hundreds of songs. It's a numbers game and often the song they go with isn't always the best song in the world. I believe the winner could sing anything and it would still be a hit because of the power of TV and the sheer number of people who sign up for it. Songwriting is an art but that is not what these shows are showcasing."

Besides his agreeability, number one success and knack for singing his own songs in tune, it was perhaps the lack of desperation about David that really won people over and marked him out as an altogether different winner. Watching the shows back, you get the sense that David enjoyed putting songs together and would have found a resourceful way of using his talents whatever the outcome of *Fame Academy*.

"David wasn't so in your face as some winners from talent shows have been," says Fraser McAlpine of BBC Chart Blog. "It was never as intense as Hear'Say's win was. It was a much more low-key affair, which seemed to be more in tone with his personality on *Fame Academy*."

Indeed. Even in publicity shots – apart from those of him residing in his chichi winner's flat – he was seen grinning with a keyboard tucked under his arm, further reminding us at home that the Yamaha was more important to him that this lofty fame business. It was music that had driven him to enter the show, music that had seen him through and music that would sustain him after all this was over. Here is a man who isn't going to chuck a toaster out of his tour bus or swear at grannies to get his face in the papers, it seemed to say. Here is a man who wants to play on his keyboard, nothing else.

Luckily enough – or unluckily for programme makers once the show had finished – he did seem to want to make music and whether the rewards of his *Fame Academy* scoop gave him that or not, it seemed he would still be grafting to find a way of getting his dream.

Perhaps this take it or leave it attitude towards fame bolstered his appeal because there are plenty of blabbering wannabes pleading

"Hello, look at me" on all kinds of reality TV programmes. David was a breath of fresh air in his steely determination to focus on the music and the music alone.

Whatever it was that had voters hooked, three million were enamoured enough to phone in and cast their ballot for David to win the first series, leaving Irish singer Sinéad Quinn (the only applicant to be chosen by the public and who at that point had beaten David Sneddon to snap up the twelfth place) and soul singer Lemar Obika as his runners up.

As winner of the Beeb show, David was handed a recording contract with Mercury Records, an Audi car and a swishy apartment in London in which he was snapped looking gleeful after his big TV win. The big flat, the ritzy car – which were on loan for a year after winning *Fame Academy* – and a million pound recording contract (whatever that means) were all his.

As nice as the flat and car package looked to the outside world they did somewhat dent the humble songwriting credentials on which *Fame Academy* built itself. Sure, songwriters should be rewarded with nice things – why not? – and there's no reason why David Sneddon shouldn't have enjoyed those perks, but for onlookers it could seem as if the prize was really the lifestyle rather than the opportunity to enjoy an illustrious career in music. It seemed to contradict the premise of the show as an opportunity for Real Musicians who wanted to play Real Music rather than a showcase for winners concerned only with the gold trappings of stardom. That said, the real clue to the show's focus is in the title.

But back to David. Once out of the *Fame Academy* barracks and in his pop star palace with his status symbol car parked outside and an impressive contract with Mercury Records, David released 'Stop Living The Lie', which still stands as the first single released by a reality/talent TV winner to have been written solely by the winner. (Although, The Cheeky Girls' self-penned – with their mum – 'Cheeky Song (Touch My Bum)', which they joyously debuted to a bemused Geri Halliwell, Pete Waterman & co on *Popstars: The Rivals* deserves a mention in that it got to number three, peaking at number two, and the week before Christmas it nestled in the top three alongside eventual winners One True Voice and Girls Aloud.) 'Stop Living The Lie' was at number one for two weeks in January 2003 and stayed in the Top 40 for a further nine weeks. Furthermore, *American Beauty* actor Kevin Spacey apparently was a big fan of the song.

Songwriter Pam Sheyne, who appeared on the first series as a songwriting mentor to David and his *Fame Academy* peers, thinks that although it's understandable why so many talent TV show winners record cover versions or songs handed to them, it would make the charts a more interesting place for music fans if more winners released self-penned songs from time to time. Or at least build up a repertoire of original songs written by other writers rather than relying on trusted covers.

In this sense, David is an anomaly in doing his own material rather than resting on the well-worn talent TV laurels. However his career has turned out since being thrust into the public eye – or however much talent TV shows may have become tarnished – he should be given props for achieving such success through his own songs.

"It is, of course, always easier to go with a well-known cover as it has an immediate sense of familiarity," says Pam Sheyne. "But there are also a number of great original hit songs being written every year and it would be nice to see people breaking with an original song more often."

Pam, who co-wrote Christina Aguilera's breakthrough hit 'Genie In A Bottle', also reckons that there's a lack of risk in the way well-known songs are covered and that the absence of individuality doesn't help music fans who might want to get a better sense of what the singer is about.

"I understand that with TV talent shows there is a sense of urgency in getting that first single out after the finals and that it is easier to choose a well-known song rather than to take a chance on an original song," says Pam. "I guess it depends on the artist and the genre of music but I would personally favour hearing a great original song to a cover because, as a listener, I want to hear something new and get a sense of who the artist is. I'd only do a cover if it was bringing something really different to the original."

Adroitly enough, 'Stop Living The Lie' gave a glimpse into the type of music that got David Sneddon fired up at that particular moment in time and helped shape out a sense of his genre and general musical trajectory. This was the style David had sculpted himself – he was no pop puppet – and, thankfully, his original piano ballad, tailored to suit him perfectly and riskily released in favour of a well-worn classic or a ditty written by someone at the label with a track record of hits, brought home the bacon. With the backing of the TV show, David achieved the highest chart ranking and his post-*Fame Academy* career seemed to have started off very well indeed.

Established as he was, David went on to push out three more Top 40 singles as well as score a Top 5 placing with his album *Seven Years – Ten Weeks*. The album featured a smattering of songs written solely by David, plus some numbers co-written with his friend and old bandmate John Kielty, and was released four months after he took the winner's title in April 2003. It was evidently a productive four months if nothing else. David even hired his beloved Elton John's band for his album, which was produced by Hugh Padgham, of Peter Gabriel and Phil Collins fame.

A whistle-stop university tour, pop roadshows around the country, a litter-picking campaign back in Scotland to reassert that the nice young man from the telly did care, a Scottish tour for home fans and appearances on comedy show *Bo Selecta!* followed, as did envy-inducing support slots for Elton John ("Elton has been my hero since I was a kid," David told *GMTV*. "Meeting him was the highlight of the year") and also rock star Bryan Adams.

To all intents and purposes David was, to borrow *Celebrity Big Brother* spawn Chantelle Houghton's phrase, living the dream. On the face of it. But 10 months after winning the show that made his name and gave him his dream career and introductions to Sir Elton, David announced that he was stepping down from the charts despite his decent whack of success.

Instead, he wanted to go back to the grindstone and his song-writing roots. The parties, TV appearances and swanky lifestyle were not for him, not what he'd got into the job for. David had attended enough celebrity parties with free booze, pastry 'nibbles' handed out by toned models and wall-to-wall with minor celebs who fill the gossip pages of newspapers and magazines to realise it wasn't really as much fun as hanging out with real friends.

With David's decision final, his management put out an explanation as to why he would turn his back on this seemingly idyllic lifestyle – which the public had voted him to have and which he seemed to want 10 short months previously. That might seem a long time to be in a job you don't feel comfortable with but giving up the role of pop star as bestowed on David Sneddon, which came with a flat, car and appearances on *Top Of The Pops,* may have been a harder pill for fans to swallow.

"He [David] was never entirely comfortable with living the life of a pop star," David's management said in a statement released after he decided to give pop the push. "He will fulfill all his live commitments, and occasionally will continue to perform, however song-writing will be his main focus."

David's own account shed a little more light on his situation. The job he was given via *Fame Academy* was great. That was the positive; the singing, piano-playing, the scribbling down songs and lyrics and the performing those songs to fans. But the negative? Just about everything else.

Despite the Noughties being the decade wherein seemingly any-one could get famous for doing nowt and make a career out of it – albeit a sabbatical into the land of celebrity or, if they're lucky long enough, to pork out on apres-nightclub snacks, then shape up and bring out a fitness video – David just wanted to be away from all that poppycock and get on with his work away from the limelight.

Refreshingly enough, he just wanted to be busy toiling at his trade and not advertising toothpaste or being papped and snapped falling out of Chinawhite at 3am with a gaggle of almost famous people. Rather than bemoan his lot, David seemed to just want to get on with a career that wouldn't be made off the back of *Fame Academy* and would allow him to get along with the things he had always set out to do. *Fame Academy* may have helped to facilitate that but rather than stick with projects spawned by the programme, he had his own career to get on with.

"I don't ever see myself being a pop star again," David told the *Daily Record*. "It's not really the life for me. I still have the fairytale. I got the job I always wanted, not just fame and fortune."

Years after his decision to hang up his pop boots and go back to writing, David would add that his change of heart about being a pop star was also due in part to the record label wanting him to write and release more piano ballads like 'Stop Living The Lie'. He'd got as far as writing his follow-up album before he realised he didn't want to pursue the piano-ballad route. Rather than go along with it for the sake of another chart-topping album that, this time, his heart wasn't in, he found something he would be passionate about doing and called time on his *Fame Academy* career before it got the better of him.

"I was close to following it through," David told *Daily Record*. "I'd been signed by Universal and was working on my second album. But one day I told my boss I hadn't really wanted to do lots of 'Stop Living A Lie'-type ballads. The record company wanted more of that, so I just decided that I didn't want to do it any more."

To most onlookers, David's decision may have seemed bizarre; after all hadn't he implored us to vote for him so he could win this dream job only a few months ago? And hadn't we spent our money calling in and pledging for him to scoop this apparent dream of his so that he could go ahead and pursue it? And hadn't all those years of trying to 'make it' and not making it made the success he achieved post-*Fame Academy* that bit sweeter? Wasn't this lifestyle the one he'd been hankering for. And didn't he realise that pop stars lived those starry lives that the rest of us could only daydream about during boring presentations at work? And couldn't he just bring out one more piano ballad album and bide his time? Apparently not.

"David Sneddon was a strange winner for *Fame Academy* in many ways," says BBC Chart Blog writer Fraser McAlpine. "He wanted to make music and when he was given a chance to, decided he didn't like everything else that came with making music, which is being a pop star and attending parties and having people be interested in what's going on in your life, and packed it all in.

"But because he never carped that much and he kept a lower profile than some of the winners do, people have either forgotten about him, don't know what he's doing nowadays because he has avoided talking about it too much and because of this, people don't seem to mock in the way it's become acceptable to do with Steve Brookstein.

"In some ways people either seem to respect him more for not biting off the hand that fed him or, because *The X Factor* is a much bigger programme, aren't so bothered that he turned his back on it."

Certainly, David never attracted the same level of fanfare as Steve Brookstein when he jacked in the *X Factor* career he was given and was allowed to just plough on with the songwriting. In Steve's defence, he was disappointed with how things turned out and the only way he could retaliate to any negative comments was by giving interviews and talking about it.

But David didn't really blast off about his gripes with *Fame Academy* or with the pop industry, other than to say, "Not for me. Thanks for the opportunity. I'll move along quietly thanks," nor did he become used as a byword for a flimsy kind of success achieved through TV. Instead, he was sort of forgotten about or, more hopefully, left to get on with his own things in peace. At worst, he may occasionally be referred to along with a string of other talent TV show winners and contestants or in a "what happened to that fella from the telly?" feature.

Needless to say, while David's pop U-turn might have been seen as wasteful – given that few people would have looked such a gift horse in the face – Fraser McAlpine acknowledges that in the long run bowing out when he did may have helped David to shed the *Fame Academy* tag and succeed on his own terms.

47

In doing so, his career has stretched out longer than one might expect for a talent TV winner who took their prize at the turn of the century before even the Crazy Frog ringtone was blasted out of every mobile phone going. That's how long ago David's win was.

Besides, if he really didn't like rest of the pop 'fairytale', better that he stepped out of the limelight while he did than moan about the perils of being a pop star at every instant. After all, who wants a pop star who continually bangs on about how awful it is being a pop star, being paid well and getting to do what you love and having lots of people like you and your music. We already have one in Eminem, thank you very much.

David's early exit from his post-*Fame Academy* career spared his fans the kick in the teeth of having him bleat about the consequences of his glittering prize and cleared the decks for other singers who did want the whole pop shebang and were willing to accept the compromises involved. Regardless of how he might have felt, it looked more dignified somehow to just say no to it all and leave it behind instead of continuing to huff and puff about how awful it all was while continuing to do the job.

"David Sneddon stepped away from any stigma *Fame Academy* and the prize he was given might have created early on," says Fraser McAlpine. "Instead, he has sort of disappeared, writing for other people and trying to get away from the whole connotations of the TV show. He never seemed at ease once he'd won *Fame Academy* and was out there trying to live the life of a pop star. He seemed more comfortable behind the keyboard then he did with the celebrity that came with his career.

"It seems that in order for a TV winner to succeed with a career on their own terms and gain respect for it, they have to dissociate themselves from the brand and start over again almost."

But David's decision to shut the door on his performing career isn't that unusual, given that *Fame Academy* seemed to attract a different breed of wannabe singers than *Pop Idol* and *Popstars.* He might have been given the golden ticket for the chocolate factory, but it didn't mean that after a year, David wouldn't get bored and come out wanting something altogether more savoury.

"*Fame Academy* seemed to lure people who seemed to take singing, music and maybe even themselves a bit more seriously," says Fraser McAlpine. "They never seem to be able to deal with being a pop star as easily as contestants on other talent shows or seem that interested in being one once they've won the show.

"Consequently, maybe fans didn't feel so peeved when David decided that he no longer wanted to be a pop star because he'd always been keen to earn his graft songwriting and so it wasn't too much of a deviation from his original aspirations. It might have seemed more like a natural progression than, say, when Steve Brookstein handed in his notice as it were, because *The X Factor* is about finding an ordinary person and making them into a superstar."

HMV head of press Gennaro Castaldo agrees that David's quick exit from the world of pop wasn't too surprising given that as the first winner of *Fame Academy*, he couldn't pore over any previous winners' CVs and hold them up as a mirror to his own. He could never have predicted if he would be suited to the life the show mapped out or at least steered him towards, and the programme makers wouldn't have known the impact the show would have in its infancy.

"The first winner of the first series of a programme is always going to have obstacles because they won't have any knowledge of how things have worked out for previous contestants and the sort of music they go on to record," says Gennaro.

"They won't know if people will enjoy watching the show and what they will be expected to do while competing on it.

"However, as the first winner, they're likely to be remembered more than any of their successors and people may give them more time because it's new, but on the flipside, they might have less idea of the sort of career that people go on to have."

Simon Hanning, who now manages *Fame Academy* series two contestant Gary Phelan, used to work as a TV producer and reckons that the fault with many talent TV programmes is that they don't offer enough in the way of guidance to contestants once the show is over, and fail to equip them with sufficient knowledge of how things might work out. No fortune tellers are needed here and who knows what's to happen in the world of pop from one day to the next, but a bit more back-up might be all students need to help steer their way towards a successful post-TV career.

Gary, whom Simon spotted at a gig at London's Cafe de Paris, is now blossoming under Simon's management and has written songs with Guy Chambers, most famous for co-crafting Robbie Williams' hits 'Angels', 'Let Me Entertain You' and 'No Regrets' among others.

Although Simon credits shows like *Fame Academy* for being peerless platforms from which to launch a pop career – especially at a time where music TV shows on terrestrial channels are few and far between and the internet is littered with wannabe musicians all vying for attention – he argues that more needs to be done once the cameras are switched off.

"My one complaint with talent TV programmes is that they do not offer any back-up afterwards to the artists taking part," he says. "We very rarely see or hear of them again. Yes the TV show is a great springboard, but you really are left to your own devices after the show is finished. Which is a very difficult place to be. Where do you go? What do you do next? These are all things that the contestants should be given advice on directly afterwards."

Perhaps, then, if more assistance had been given to David Sneddon – and especially other *Fame Academy* contestants who don't have the mollycoddling enjoyed by the winner – in the aftermath of the show ending, they wouldn't have fallen off the radar so quickly or wouldn't have become disillusioned with the path their working lives were heading towards.

Maybe rather than just seeing the whopping great launch pad stretched out in front of them, contestants and their mentors should really be thinking of the end game and not just who will win the competition, get the flat and get their mug in one of the floating bubbles that introduce *Friday Night With Jonathan Ross*.

On the upside, *X Factor* contestant Austin Drage thinks that although TV shows like *Fame Academy* and *The X Factor* offer new singers unrivalled exposure to the public, being able to play instruments and understand music is priceless for a long-term future and of all the programmes, *Fame Academy* offered the most support in this area.

While many contestants might have angelic singing voices, 'star quality' and may be able to shake their booties like Beyoncé, Austin thinks that the one thing that should reassure David Sneddon or any other contestant with musical aptitude is that being able to piece a tune together offers wider scope for opportunities if your post-TV career dries up.

As such Austin thinks it's especially useful for talent scouts to be able to see footage of contestants playing instruments and being able to tell their flats from their sharps so that they keep them in mind for future work unsuited to untrained TV contestants. Also, being able to play means that the contestant can exert more control over their musical direction because they have more confidence in what style works best for them. Having these extra skills marks you out from every other contestant. It gives you the X Factor. David, take heed.

"The one thing that is really sad for me is that no one expects you to have any knowledge of music or what you're doing when you've been on a show like *The X Factor*," says Austin. "They expect you just to be a puppet on a string and it's quite upsetting because they don't realise that you do write, you do play and you do understand how to piece together a song, but that's overlooked because they don't see enough of it, which is a shame.

"But you know these things when you enter *The X Factor*, you know that people are never shown playing instruments and that it is more about singing. That said, if I sit down and play a keyboard or a set of drums people will be taken by surprise and say, 'Oh I didn't know you could play'. Well they never showed me playing instruments on *The X Factor*, which is why you didn't know that I could play.

"If you look at Dave Grohl, he played drums in Nirvana, sang and played guitar in Foo Fighters and now he's back drumming for

Them Crooked Vultures. He's a great drummer, great frontman and a great guitarist.

"People don't get to see that on *The X Factor. The X Factor* has a lot of positives about it and it pushes you out into the public domain, which is really helpful, but it would be great if they could show someone like that on the show who can play, who knows how to perform and write different sorts of music and who can really diversify. To me, that's someone who is an inspiration.

"I think they should give contestants instruments on *The X Factor* like they did on *Fame Academy*. Show them practising through the weeks. I think kids at home and loads of people I know would be much more excited to see someone playing guitar and improving than just seeing someone sing. Every boy at school wants to be a lead guitarist in a band.

"As such it'd be nice to see a bloke pick up a guitar and start playing it while he's in *The X Factor*. Because if you come out just with your singing voice that's great, but your style of singing might not be enough once you're out of the show.

"People might not want your particular style. If you have musical talent in other areas I think it helps you out in the long run and I think it gives you more chance of having a longer career and certainly one where people respect the fact that you know what you're talking about when it comes to music. You might have a lot to learn and you might need other people to help you along the way but at least you understand the basics.

"That's why David Sneddon could leave his singing behind but still have a career in music writing for other people. *Fame Academy* might have helped put him in touch with the right people and get his work known but it's his training in music that has helped him hold on to his songwriting career.

"If you have those skills you can produce for people, write for them. Look at Will.I.Am. He writes for other people like Cheryl Cole, produces, writes for Black Eyed Peas, raps and sings. Prince writes and produces his own material. Mark Ronson has produced for so many established acts.

"If more people coming off these shows could do it then they might have longer careers than they currently have because then they have the versatility to do so, plus they'll know the right people from being involved in the show. I think it'd be brilliant if *The X Factor* did that alongside what they already do because they would attract different contestants."

Consequently, David Sneddon appears to have played his *Fame Academy* cards very sensibly indeed, and his manner of handling things can be regarded as a template for any future talent TV programme contestants.

He enjoyed songwriting, had always enjoyed it and was shown enjoying doing so while on *Fame Academy*. He became known for his love of songwriting once out in the world of pop. He had a chance to be the frontman, didn't like it and went back to songwriting, using some of the contacts he'd acquired from his *Fame Academy* days, a move that made him look more genuine as a serious musician. He never really bad-mouthed the programme that made his name and instead just knuckled down and found a way to make a success of himself his way.

And coming talent TV full circle, David and his songwriting partner Jay Bauer-Mein signed a deal with Syco, Simon Cowell's record label, and Sony to write songs for artists like *Pop Idol's* very own Will Young. Although he does admit that his route to success has been quite unusual for the TV contestant ilk.

Besides his contract with Syco, David's self-scribed song 'Baby Get Higher' was covered by Dutch singer Van Velzen and he has also written tracks for soul singer Nate James. "I've taken a bizarre route to become a songwriter," David told *Paisley Daily Express*. "I don't think there's been another reality TV winner who took a back step to this side of the industry but I like just being allowed to get on with my work.

"It's a massive opportunity. To an extent, this is a bigger achievement than winning *Fame Academy*. To become a respected songwriter is something I've wanted for 15 years. At the same time, winning *Fame Academy* was a massive thing for me. It totally changed my life. I would still like to think that I would have got to the point where I am now without *Fame Academy*, but probably not as quick."

Series two contestant Gary Phelan, who has since released his own single 'Pillar To Post', reckons that David at least gave his winners' career a chance, whereas some winners expect too much of the show and don't bother with the opportunity they're handed. "I think David Sneddon did the best with what he had and I think it's good that he's got back to doing what he wants to do with performing at gigs and songwriting," says Gary.

"Sometimes people don't make the best of the opportunity they've been given, even Alex Parks, who won the second series. But I think with David Sneddon it's good that he's gone back to doing something he loves even if it isn't talked about as much as his music was after leaving the programme."

While David has taken a backstage role in pop and has since turned his fortunes around to reach a position he is comfortable with, his peers have become more famous than him. One of those peers, Lemar, is so successful now that his first name is enough for people to recognise him. Madonna, Sting, Kylie, Lemar. That's how far the lad's come.

Londoner Lemar had already had plenty of experience in pop before he entered the first series of *Fame Academy*. At 17, after years of singing Jackson 5 numbers with his siblings at home he scored a support slot for R&B champ Usher at a concert in Tottenham. He was offered a place to study pharmacy at Cardiff University but gave it up to pursue music and supported top-notch performers like Destiny's Child as well as the sharp-suited Usher before getting a recording deal with BMG.

He recorded a single – 'Got Me Singing Ooh' – which carried a sort of UK garage vibe that was popular at the time it was written in 2001. Unfortunately it was shelved and Lemar was dropped after a reshuffle at the label. A short spell working in the Enfield NatWest bank as an account manager followed but Lemar was still set on turning his singing talent into a full-time career. Knowing about standing orders may be useful but pop was more alluring. Still, isn't it

Hear today ... Gone tomorrow: Hear'Say at the height of their fame as a band.
(*ITV/Rex Features*)

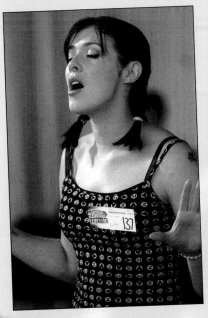

Popstar ... Kym Marsh singing for a place in the *Popstars* band. (*ITV/Rex Features*)

Number one ... Hear'Say member Danny Foster recalls the group's chart success. (*Herbie Knott/Rex Features*)

Say it again ... Hear'Say celebrate after getting the highest number of sales for a debut single in chart history. (*Ken McKay/Rex Features*)

Being Simm-body ... Liberty X member Kevin Simm auditioning for a place in the *Popstars* band. *(ITV/Rex Features)*

The Heat is on ... Liberty X member Michelle Heaton practices her dance moves in an audition for *Popstars*. *(ITV/Rex Features)*

Doin' It ... *Popstars* runners up Liberty X launch a pop career after losing out on places in the *Popstars* band. *(Nils Jorgensen/Rex Features)*

Girl alone ... Cheryl Cole (nee Tweedy)
at her audition for *Popstars: The Rivals*.
(ITV/Rex Features)

Tongue hot summer ... Girls Aloud member
Sarah Harding at her audition for *Popstars:
The Rivals*. (ITV/Rex Features)

Plait's the way to do it ... Girls Aloud
member Nicola Roberts at her audition for
*Popstars: The Rivals*. (ITV /Rex Features)

Chosen ... Girls Aloud member Nadine Coyle
at her audition for *Popstars: The Rivals*.
(ITV/Rex Features)

Bye boys... Kimberley Walsh, Sarah Harding, Nicola Roberts, Nadine Coyle and Cheryl Cole celebrate forming their band Girls Aloud. *(Ken McKay/Rex Features)*

After You're Gone ... Short-lived boy band One True Voice who were the winning male band on *Popstars: The Rivals*. (*ITV/Rex Features*)

Dave Academy ... *Fame Academy* winner David Sneddon puts in some time on the keyboard. [*Rex Features*]

The beautiful Fame ... contestants from the first series of *Fame Academy* outside the hallowed music mansion.
[*Alex Lentati/Evening Standard/Rex Features*]

Quick, think of something witty to say! ... Alex Parks, winner of the second series of *Fame Academy*, finds herself at the centre of press attention after being named the winner. [*Richard Austin/Rex Features*]

Don't Give It Up ... Hugely successful *Fame Academy* runner up Lemar Obika. (*Rex Features*)

good to know that a pop star could also advise you on the best rates on current accounts after singing a couple of hits?

Still keen on chasing that elusive music dream, Lemar entered *Fame Academy*. Scoring a duet – 'Easy (Like Sunday Morning)' – with Lionel Richie and covering Al Green songs, he fast became known for his dulcet renditions and for being a fine soul vocalist, which sent out signals to the right people that soul was his bag and he would very much like to find his calling in songs such as those featured on the show.

"I'm just glad people have taken to my voice. I just try to express the words and bring out the emotion in the song," said Lemar during *Fame Academy*.

That he did. While Lemar was popular during his time on the BBC programme, he would eventually lose out to Irish singer Sinéad Quinn and David Sneddon and came third over all. After being booted out in the semi-finals, it wasn't long before Wolverhampton singer Beverley Knight – who'd heard Lemar on the show – got in touch to ask him to perform a duet with her at a gig in Hammersmith.

Then Sony signed Lemar to a five-year contract, and he made an album, *Dedicated*, which won him fans and support among the critics.

"It's a shame for David Sneddon whom most people have forgotten. You could walk past him in the street and not know who he is and it's the same for Leon Jackson who won *The X Factor,*" says former *X Factor* contestant Austin Drage. "But on the other hand, David Sneddon might not have liked being recognised anyway so it might work to his favour. Yet you get someone like Lemar from the same show as David, who came third, and his career has gone the complete opposite way.

"He came out of *Fame Academy*, took some time and wrote a cracking album, came back and everyone loved him. It happened for him. It's really crazy. Coming out of a show like *Fame Academy* or *The X Factor* as a runner-up can work out or it can bite you on the bum.

"It's a doubled-edged sword: do you win the show and get

pushed in a direction you don't want to go and have to suck it up, or do you come second and have the chance of not being known after the programme's over but have more control over your direction and consequently fly into success or, without the big label backing, into obscurity?"

Happily, Lemar saw his third-place ranking as a boon and, without the pressure of the big win that David Sneddon may have experienced, was able to work on his tunes a little while longer and finely tune his performances and direction until everything was just so. In doing this, he also lost the ex-*Fame Academy* performer tag and was able to shape a career on his own terms.

"I just took my time to write songs, I had the time to work with producers and work on my act for six or seven months – that was the bonus of not winning the show," Lemar told the BBC in 2004.

It might have helped that, besides not having the weight of expectations a winner might have placed upon them and the time to perfect his sound, Lemar brought out an R&B album, which according to HMV spokesperson Gennaro Castaldo is also a fruitful move.

"R&B and pop ballads always tend to do incredibly well in the charts," says Gennaro. "They tend to get lots of radio airplay and time on TV, which is all-important now that there are few regular dedicated music programmes. They tap into the stations and TV channels and get out there. It's a very popular genre and it doesn't suffer as much as some other genres that fall out of favour quickly."

Daniel DeBourg, who entered *The X Factor* in series four and has since gone on to have a successful career in dance music and managing other acts including fellow *X Factor* contestants Miss Frank, reckons that Lemar's success came down to his well-thought-out songs. "Lemar had a bit more time to work on his album and when he released his singles it was almost like he'd never been on *Fame Academy*," says DeBourg. "He almost went back underground. He didn't just release a cover or something quick and easy while people still knew his name, he brought out music that suited him and that he and the people around him believed in.

"That's why he's still going… because he works at his music and doesn't just bring out a single for the sake of it."

Talking of which, Lemar's first single since leaving *Fame Academy*, 'Dance With U', went to number two in the charts when it was released in 2003 and later, in 2004, he scooped up a Brit award for best urban act. Lemar has done so well for himself since leaving the BBC programme that he was even one of the acts – including The Darkness and Travis – on the cobbled together Band Aid 20 version of 'Do They Know It's Christmas?' brought out in 2004.

Lemar's mantlepiece has been kept in gongs since stepping out of the airwaves. He picked up another Brit in 2006 for Best Urban Brit – again! – and he had the honour of being the ninth richest reality TV star in the Noughties, just wedged between *Big Brother* handyman Craig Phillips and former cruise-singing Wakefield diva Jane McDonald from BBC's docu-soap *The Cruise*.

If you're wondering how much moolah Lemar had accrued in his time on *Fame Academy* to be deemed as the ninth wealthiest, his estimated wealth is around the £4m mark. On top of that he's had a charity boxing match with *GMTV's* Ben Shephard. And just to cement Lemar's position as an established, respected musician, he's even got a greatest hits album to his name.

Still, Lemar, who has since taken *X Factor* runners-up JLS under his wing and offered them the support slot on his UK tour, is nevertheless careful about maintaining a good profile after coming out of talent TV shows. Tellingly, he reckons the hardest part comes after fleeing *Fame Academy* and programmes of its ilk. That's when people can quickly forget you as the latest bright sparks enter similar competitions and grab the limelight.

"The public embrace you at the beginning but forget the telly show quickly," Lemar said in an interview. "You've got to keep them hugging and give them good stuff and good stuff regularly. I told them [JLS] the key is to keep your head down and work like you've never worked before. The hardest thing is getting a break, luckily for them they got it."

Likewise, JLS were similarly aware that times can be tough for extalent TV show contestants once their mugs are off the TV every week. "You have to admire Lemar for his staying power. He didn't even win *Fame Academy,* I can't remember where he came but it wasn't first or second or anything like that but he's still here," says JLS singer Marvin.

"There's not many people who have come off reality TV programmes [and done really well], there's only Lemar and Leona and Will Young, I would say, and Girls Aloud. They're probably the only top tour acts that have had the real staying power for being proper artists. So you have to admire that in him."

While Lemar is arguably the most well-known and long-serving pop star from *Fame Academy*, his peers have also maintained careers in music. Runner-up Sinéad Quinn scored a number two song with her single 'I Can't Break Down', which was kept off the top spot by Russian pop duo t.A.T.u.'s angsty teen anthem 'All The Things She Said'.

Since bringing out her single and debut album, *Ready To Run*, Sinéad has entertained troops the world over, formed a new band, Sinéad & The Dawnbreakers, and married the drummer from soft rock band The Feeling.

Katie Lewis, a contestant on the first series, remains positive about her experience of the show. Since leaving, she performed in a girl group, Unleashed, and has now gone back to solo work. Katie insists that *Fame Academy* gave her an unrivalled introduction to the inner workings of the music industry and helped point her in the right direction. She's since been working on a rock and opera sound, a little like emo-wailers Evanescence, and is still enthusiastic about making music.

"Since *Fame Academy* I've spent a lot of time writing and recording," says Katie. "I was in a girl band for three years, which allowed me to tour all over the world, so I was basically just out gaining experience and working out my style. *Fame Academy* helped me massively because I was very young and it opened a lot of doors for me. It was also an amazing experience.

"I was about to start auditioning for drama school as I wanted to be an actress and had come to the end of my college course so *Fame Academy* was just a trial audition but I never imagined it would lead to what it did."

Katie reckons that talent TV shows have changed and the type of contestant they attract is different now from the early days when a man in a roll-neck singing Britney Spears and snapping his fingers at the cameras was considered shocking. As such, Katie says that the extraneous drama can detract from talent.

"I think reality TV is very different from what it was when it all began. It's not just about talent any more," she says. "I don't think people are always taken seriously afterwards but it depends on the person and talent."

However successful some acts on talent TV shows can become, Katie also thinks that for some, their time in pop can be very short if they don't make an impact – and enough money – early on, which in turn can be damaging to a new singer. "There are some people that come from those shows like Leona Lewis and Jennifer Hudson for example who are amazing and will always be successful. But there are others that get spat out very quickly because they don't make the fat cats enough money and it could be awful for them and also the end of their career if they let it. So it just depends but any-one who goes on those shows should know it's the chance they take.

"I'm glad I went on *Fame Academy* because it was a great intro-duction to the music industry, I had some amazing experiences and met some amazing people and learned so much but I can also see why it's not the same for everyone. For me the programme was very much the beginning of my career."

So while things worked out swimmingly for Katie, Lemar and even David in the end, let's now move on to series two.

# Chapter 4

# *Fame Academy* Series Two

With one series of *Fame Academy* in the bag and a spin-off in the form of *Comic Relief Does Fame Academy* out of the way, *Fame Academy* was fully established and part of the TV fabric when the second series hit the airwaves.

The second series came just seven months after first series winner David 'Snedders' Sneddon had won the show and promised to feed our hungry charts with new talent discovered before our very eyes. Handily, since David had decided to give frontline pop a miss, there was room in 2003 for a new batch of *Fame Academy* contestants.

After all, there isn't infinite time and space in the charts and on radio playlists for every talent TV contestant going, so with David bowing out, space was opened up for new faces from *Fame Academy* and, as far as possible, give another expectant pop hopeful the chance to wear the *Fame Academy* badge a bit longer.

Head of press for HMV Gennaro Castaldo thinks that the quick turnover of talent TV contestants means that, besides battling it out with other chart newcomers, they have to release records as soon as they can while people remember them. And with every passing series, the competition between the ex-contestants will get fiercer.

Lucky then that David was looking for his way out at that point when the new students appeared on screen.

"Contestants on *Fame Academy, The X Factor* and TV searches for stars often find that once they release singles, they are up against not just their peers from their series but also all the past competitors and likewise ex-contestants from similar shows," says Gennaro.

"It's the nature of the programmes but it means that after your series has ended you only have a short space of time before the next batch of contestants bring out their singles and, with the best will in the world, some of those contestants will get lost in the charts because if they don't have a strong enough song to rely on to grab music fans' attentions, it's likely that interest in them will wane.

"This is because it's probable that their back story will be the same as all the other ex-contestants and any more interesting quirks will be known about from going on the programme, so it can be hard for them to sustain interest and to differentiate the contestants. That does happen with singers who haven't been on a TV talent show but have found their style become popular.

"What ex-contestants do have in their favour is that people recognise them and know their style before they listen to any releases because they've seen them on TV and have heard what type of music they like to perform. But their problem is that they have to hold that attention and make their music a more powerful brand than their association with the TV show, because so many other acts in the charts will have that too so they have to make themselves unique."

Thus with David Sneddon out of the way and many of the students from his year's series scurrying off to make albums and keeping out of the way of the Top 5, the second series started with a pretty clean slate.

Songwriter Pam Sheyne appeared as a tutor during the first series of *Fame Academy*. Although fond of the students, Pam decided not to return for the second series and agrees that the high production rate of new talent unearthed on TV talent searches means that ex-contestants often fade into the background quickly unless they grab the public's attention at the time. "People are only interested in who won the last show, they move on very quickly to the next thing," says Sheyne.

She thinks that often TV talent programmes are dressed up as shows designed to cultivate and promote talent but this is largely a footnote compared with the desire to captivate audiences and drive ratings up. Singing 'Kum Ba Yah' on an acoustic guitar probably isn't going to make as exciting telly as someone snogging a fellow contestant and then being cheeky to a mentor.

"The general public is not going to remember who won a talent show six years ago unless they are in the public eye now," she says. "TV talent shows give everybody who thinks they are 'anybody' the chance of making their dreams come true. They may sell it to the public as a 'nurturing talent and developing careers' kind of show but they are there essentially to entertain people and to get ratings."

So *Fame Academy* series two came around and followed this sort of entertaining trajectory (but still carried on mentioning the talent they were nurturing at any given opportunity – such is life). Music was still an essential part of the show's foundation but plenty of drama was added to the mix to keep viewers riveted to their sets, compelled to watch week after week to keep up with the progress of the students.

Maintaining this air of the new and the dramatic, headmaster Richard Park wiped off any lingering smiles from the first series that could be deemed too kindly and encouraging and pulled out a range of damning scowls and cleverly crafted put-downs such as, "He reminded me of the Incredible Hulk getting out of the suit" and "If this boy makes it to the big time, he'll have a very nice life" – for the second series. He'd evidently got wind of Simon Cowell's initially much-maligned but gradually respected and fully embraced 'Mr Nasty' persona by now.

The change in attitude upped the drama ante and gave the series more of the soap opera feel that had been well-received on *Pop Idol*, at that point showing on ITV. But to balance this stern style out and, presumably, for added credibility, Robin Gibb of The Bee Gees stepped up as a judge for the live shows and usually offered some timely feedback to the students after they'd performed.

Richard, who despite having plenty of musical accolades to his name, famous friends (of which he spoke frequently – "I knew Karen Carpenter you know," he said in an interview with *The Times*) and a well-tuned ear, was positioned as the one who'd bring any errant student down a peg or two, while programme host Patrick Kielty often spoke over Richard or tried to stifle his over-the-top criticism. In a very non-BBC family entertainment moment, Richard was caught on camera mouthing the word 'wanker' to Patrick during the celebrity spin-off of the show, an incident that prompted 450 complaints.

The two came to verbal blows over Richard's critique of James Fox's performance one week, with dean of pop Richard becoming infuriated when his comments were drowned out by Patrick's own take on the contestant's cover version of John Lennon's 'Woman'.

"Appalling," said Richard. Boo sucks (or something to that effect) retaliated Patrick. The bad feeling between the pair meant they were moved to dressing rooms that were further apart and stopped going on jollies together outside of the show. Even so, the spat was dissed in the press as a staged brouhaha to pull in more viewers. Not so, said the gents who seemed happy in the knowledge that they'd both thrown their toys out of the pram in front of millions of people.

"Patrick Kielty is there to host the show," said Richard Park at the time. "But he is too desperate to voice an opinion, too desperate to side with the artist, too desperate to side with the people in the audience."

(Four years down the line, Patrick would turn his rage towards Sutton Coldfield-born co-presenter Cat Deeley, who darted off to America to host light entertainment programmes over there instead of hanging around to console and congratulate Colin Murray, Linda Robson and the other famous faces appearing on *Comic Relief Does Fame Academy* 2007. Why ever would she do that eh? "If she wants to make vast sums of money in one of the few countries that didn't sign up to the trade agreement, then she doesn't care about aid at all," he told *The Sun*. "I'm glad I'm hosting with Claudia Winkleman now. It's good to be working with someone who wants to be here. Cat's turned her back on us. Good luck to her and her capitalism." Er right, that told her.)

While Patrick and Richard bawled each other out and took the attention away from the contestants, Robin Gibb – and co-judges Carrie and David Grant, who also taught the students how to sing and often found themselves at odds with Richard's critiques – became a voice of reason and a calming influence over the nervy contestants, dispensing pearls of wisdom with a supportive smile.

Later, Robin would be repaid by the students when they covered Bee Gees songs for a collection packaged up as a *Fame Academy Bee Gees Special* album after the series had ended. (Surely it can't be long before enthusiastic *X Factor* hopefuls, armed with posters of young Dannii Minogue playing sulky tomboy Emma in Aussie soap *Home And Away*, will be warbling out 'Love And Kisses', 'Su$$ess' and 'Put The Needle On It' – or even 'I Begin To Wonder', complete with sign language for extra kudos – in a long-awaited Dannii Minogue special, complete with a spin-off album. Watch this space.)

With the decks cleared in the charts for the new *Fame Academy* hopefuls to launch themselves after the show had ended, a new style of judge – even if he had been on the previous year's series – and a well-respected Bee Gee in the pack, the second series was ready for the drama to be cranked up good and proper.

That included letting the public choose between 25 wannabes all vying for a place in the *Academy* every week until the 13 students were picked. Again, once that pop baker's dozen was selected, the public were encouraged to phone in their vote for their favourite performers each week in the live showdowns where the students had to sing to the audience.

The votes were then totted up and the three least popular singers – those who'd received the fewest number of votes from the public – were informed of their fate on the live TV show and placed in the precarious position of having to plead with the judges to let them stay. One out of the three losing contestants would then be picked by the judges to go through to the next round, usually after much skittish deliberation from the panel over who best deserved to come back the following week to prove they'd taken their advice on board. This was the decade of 'taking it on board' after all.

Then it was up to the remaining students to decide. Taking it on board wouldn't matter to them as much. It was more about who 'wanted it' the most. This was also the decade of 'wanting it so badly' after all. Those same fellow students with whom they, the nervy pair waiting to learn their fate, had all become fast friends; indeed, they were all like a big family, their brothers and sisters, which is why deciding who out of the two contestants left on the shelf would go through to next week's competition was the hardest decision they'd ever had to make.

The contestant who wasn't chosen by the judges or their fellow contestants would be told to hop it, causing much nail-biting, teary outbursts and momentary distress for contestants and viewers alike. And then the whole process would start over the following week.

The pumped-up drama and emotional, elongated elimination rounds often involved high-octane blubbing and faltering declarations along the lines of "This person is so brilliant and I really wish I didn't have to do this. In fact, I can't believe I've been made to do this. This is so unfair. This is so hard but based on that performance I'm voting them out. I'm so sorry. Can we just stop this now?" All of this, of course, meant that there was less time to show the contestants writing songs or, at very least, singing them.

Actually getting to grips with how to write songs and play instruments and improve on their skills in this area was something that was touched on much later in the series when there was only a handful of singers left. Presumably, with many of the hopefuls gone, having time to write a song might spare them the tedium that ex-contestant Nick Hall said was spent, "Trying to think of things to do while the cameras watched us," with just "30 minutes of music therapy a day" in the earlier stages of the competition to keep them on the straight and narrow. That's to say, keep them focused on 'the dream'.

Thus, even in *Fame Academy*, the balance between music and

drama shifted in favour of drama, leaving music as a side issue. Music was all well and good but watching a group of people hungry to sing and perform write a song isn't as interesting as watching them playing teen party favourite Truth or Dare or seeing the headmaster and presenter get in a barney with them. Add to the drama the fact that the only contact the contestants could have with the outside world was performing in the live showdowns week after week to an audience of *Holby City* actors, some family members and the hard-to-impress judging panel, plus a three-minute phone call back home to air gripes about being a *Fame Academy* student and remind mum to record *EastEnders,* and you have a lot of ballyhoo and little musical output on your hands.

There were greater theatrics in the outside world when the second series moved from a Friday night – where they once lost out in a ratings battle with ITV who scooped a bigger audience for the forgettable Julia Roberts and Richard Gere film *Runaway Bride* – to a Saturday where they went directly up against ITV's mighty popular *Pop Idol.* The move, which some saw as a cynical ploy purely to drive up viewing figures and compete with ITV, was even discussed in the parliamentary review of the BBC's charter and moved the show further towards drama and disagreements than actually singing, making music and discovering new talent.

Outside of the debating chambers, some of the contestants were peeved with the new-look programme. Indeed, a gripe that series two contestant Gary Phelan found with the new suspenseful format was not that it was going against the Beeb's values or that it was primarily concerned with just trying to pull in more viewers rather than offer quality TV, it was more that the melodrama was clearly designed to overshadow the music that it was supposed to care about so much.

The drama and lengthy evictions from the *Academy* left little time for students to be seen perfecting their songwriting skills and when they did get a chance to sing, they had little say over which songs they wanted to sing, which ultimately meant they could be presented as a completely different style of performer from the type they preferred. Singing covers on a prominent prime-time show might be great experience but Gary had hoped that he would have more help with improving his musical abilities. Sensibly, he realised that learning those skills would give him a great foundation from which to build a sustainable career.

Even the choice of song a contestant wanted to sing could be changed to one they cared little about, just to ensure a balance of styles of music on the programme. "When you start out in the pro-gramme you're asked to put forward a list of about nine or 10 songs that you wanted to sing, which is good because at least you have control of the type of songs you would like to sing and you can put down songs that you really love and which mean something to you and that makes all the difference," says Gary. "But basically, because they wanted to make *Fame Academy* appealing across the board and make sure that everyone was picking something different, you'd have to each keep off one another's patch.

"They needed the songs we sang in the show to cover all bases and appeal to everyone watching and all their varying tastes because it was a family show and not just for one demographic. In fairness to them, I can see the point of this; you can't have everyone singing Robbie Williams songs in the exact style of Robbie Williams. It would be dull for viewers and dull for contestants.

"However, I struggled with that because every time I picked something different, I had to choose something else so we were each recognisable and had a distinctive style so that people would be able to get used to us and so that we didn't crossover with each other. They didn't want people singing songs that were too similar to each other – which might be feasible on a TV show but it's not so realis-tic for the charts."

To make sure there was a sizeable quota of varying music on that show, on the week he left the programme Gary had the misfortune to perform a song with which he had no emotional connection. Gary's song – a Corrs number – evidently filled the tin whistle and folk pop quota but it wasn't remotely like anything he'd shown inter-est in singing while on the show.

That aside, he'd never heard of the song before he was asked to sing it and despite knowing that singing different styles expands your range, didn't feel it would be that beneficial to him. As a young singer with little prior experience of the music industry, he felt it best to button up and sing it because he didn't want to come across as bolshy and wouldn't accept advice from those who'd been in the business longer than he. Unfortunately, the song was the last he sang on the show.

"The song I went out on by The Corrs I'd never even heard before," he says. "It wasn't the right song for me and I would rather have sang I song I knew and loved because I feel I would have performed it better. But when you're in a show like that you do what you're told because it's a great opportunity and you don't want to upset anybody or make like you know best. You know you're a beginner and that other people have been doing music longer than you, so you accept their advice because they have more experience than you. You don't want to bite the hand that feeds you."

Gary, who has worked with Robbie Williams's songwriter of choice, Guy Chambers, since leaving the show, has finally found a direction in which he wants to take his music with the help of his manager Simon Hanning. After he was given his marching orders from *Fame Academy* he has been given far more command over the type of music he records and is content with his career. "I think as well as not always wanting to sing the songs I was given, I was struggling with what I wanted to do and which direction I wanted to go in and I needed help in that area," he says.

"I was in a boy band before *Fame Academy* and wanted to be more serious so you see the transition on the show. But it's only now I'm out of the show that I've started to find the music I really like. That's been helped so much by my manager, Simon, who really understands what music suits me best. But on *Fame Academy,* you're just basically being told what to sing and you're not getting much control over it."

So Gary and his peers scuttled off trying to make themselves decidedly different from one another; he's pop, she's angst pop, he's rock, she's indie and so on until all areas of the chart spectrum were filled.

Perhaps the most dramatic result of the programme, putting aside the melodrama of the live showdowns and antics from the students, was that yet again the legacy of David Sneddon hung over the winner. Series two's elected winner, Alex Parks, turned her back on the fame that was whipped up by winning the show almost as soon as she left the studios after being handed her glittering prize.

Not only that, but she has turned her back on the *Fame Academy* brand entirely or at least become dissociated with it through her career choices. Much like her predecessor David Sneddon, about whom she claimed to have no awareness after her win, things would be different for her. "I don't know anything about David and have never met him," she said after her win. "This year it would have been very different no matter who had won."

And so it was that Alex, undeterred by David handing in his notice at pop's door, came to the nation's attention through *Fame Academy*. A fresh-faced 19-year-old singer from Mount Hawke, Cornwall when she appeared on the show, Alex grew up listening to Elvis and Michael Jackson and made her first public appearance singing aged 13 at a school concert. Before *Fame Academy* was on the airwaves, Alex won a songwriting competition and £2,000 for her song 'To You', which she performed with One Trick Pony, a band she sang in at that time.

Even so, Alex didn't think she'd stand much of a shot at being selected for *Fame Academy*, let alone winning the show. Fortunately people around her did. Encouraged by her dad, she applied and was selected as a finalist. Alex had studied clown skills and physical theatre at drama school, been on the dole for a bit, performed with the local drama group and was trying to work out what next to do, much like many people of that age.

She'd played in bands and had given songwriting a go – and evidently had found some local success with it – but she didn't feel she had the confidence – or was methodical enough – to get a demo together, to apply and go on the telly and give her music a wider platform. "I saw that the show was coming back on, and I remember thinking, 'I wonder if I could do something like that?'" she told *The Guardian* in 2003. "But I'm really disorganised, so I just wouldn't have been planned enough to send a tape off. I didn't think there was any point, so I didn't do it."

Happily her dad did see the point and sent in a video of his daughter performing. Soon enough, Alex was entered into the show and selected as one of the 25. With much anxious waiting around, Alex was the last of all wannabes to sing for her supper and had to contend with tonsillitis while singing 'Beautiful' by Christina Aguilera to earn her place in the *Academy*. The judges and public were impressed by her talent – and undeterred by her throat infection and nerves or perhaps beguiled by her determination to sing despite this – and selected her as one of the finalists for the show.

Once fully enrolled in *Fame Academy,* Alex quickly gained support from famous fans as well as viewers with her heartfelt covers of Coldplay, Tracy Chapman and Christina Aguilera songs delivered in her distinct voice. She seemed determined to focus on her singing and not make a song and dance about her sexuality in order to rouse interest in her. Her talent did the talking for her. ("That's [my sexuality] just me. I didn't come in here trying to hide it or shout about it," she said on the show. "Concentrating on writing and singing is what I'm looking forward to now.")

Adored by Jonathan Ross ("That was up there with just about everyone I have ever seen," said Rossy of Alex's final performance on the show), Lenny Henry and Daniel Bedingfield – who spoke of Alex's "unique and special" talent during the live final and urged viewers to vote her as the winner, which some criticised as there was little similar support for the other two finalists – Alex was à la mode with three of the best-selling singers of that time, Pink, Christina Aguilera and Avril Lavigne, all of whom were never slow in mentioning how uncompromising they were with their music when asked.

Even Radiohead, ordinarily the least likely of groups to take an interest in popular TV talent searches and who certainly wouldn't appear in the audience at these showdowns, stepped up to praise Alex's talent when they appeared on Radio 1. Naturally, however, they were concerned at the way in which someone of her calibre should have to be discovered on TV to get noticed and the consequences for new artists who were discovered this way.

"She's got a fucking great voice and if this is the only way she can get out to people it's a shame because there's really something going on there and people will dismiss it because it's that," said the band in the interview with the youth radio show. "If that's the only way to get exposed now then there's something seriously wrong with the music industry. I'm against the safety of it all. The industry sort of eating itself whole seems to be depressingly pointless."

Even though Alex's singing forte was brought to wider attention via the telly, she certainly wasn't the type of in-yer-face fame-seeker associated with the TV genre that made her name. Her antics were much more subdued than many of the contestants who played Truth or Dare, back-chatted Richard Park, snogged each other, got trollied and stripped to their shirts.

Alex's most impish moment came when she rocked up 20 minutes late, dishevelled and half-asleep to an exercise lesson with the *Academy's* fitness instructor, Kevin Adams, who gave her a telling off in front of her peers. She soon bounced back from his public chiding and carried on with the exercise class. But while no troublemaker, Alex was also no wallflower on the programme and in the immediate aftermath of her win frequently had her name prefixed with 'angsty', suggesting that she could stick up for herself and wasn't about to be told exactly what to do. Which turned out to be a pretty accurate summation.

She expressed doubts in her abilities throughout her two months in the show (doubtless this was genuine concern for the singer but even so, showing a little humility seems to go a long way in TV searches for singing talent because there can only be so many big-heads in every series), pointing to a fragility that might have endeared fans, especially as her niggling worries about not being good enough were unfounded when they voted her as their winner. Nevertheless, Alex won over more than just Bedders and Ross; she was the bookies' favourite from the first episode after the 13 finalists were selected and eventually scooped the main prize.

After winning the show Alex even pointed out that her two runners up, Carolynne Good and Alistair Griffin, were much more straight-up pop and more in the model of the self-assured pop star than she was at that moment. She thought every other contestant would win over her and was shown looking completely surprised by the win. "My legs were like jelly after the first two songs and I just got it back together to keep performing. I was so overwhelmed I was worried my voice wouldn't come out," she said on the show after being told she was the winner.

"It was amazing to win, I really didn't expect it. I always thought Paris (Campbell-Edwards) would win. I know it will be really hard to keep grounded but I don't want to change and hopefully it won't go to my head."

Still in shock at her win and determined to keep that head free of gushing adulation and remain grounded, once Alex had regained composure of her legs she made it clear that she didn't give two hoots for the lifestyle that came with being a pop star and that she wanted her singing career to be based on much more than a throwaway cover or two and a few appearances on red carpets at film premieres.

Her heartfelt covers performed on the show, self-drafted songs and wide-ranging influences – Annie Lennox, Sinéad O'Connor and Ani DiFranco, who have all gone on to success while keeping their candour, a route seemingly attractive to Alex – seemed to speak of someone who cared more for the craft of singing and songwriting than the celebrity and added extras that seemed so attractive to too many other wannabe stars who filled the pages of celebrity magazines that decade.

Like David Sneddon before her, Alex also won a lavish flat in London – this time in pretty nifty Notting Hill – and as well as a BMW sports car, some bottles of Bolly and the all-important recording contract. One week after winning the prime-time Beeb pro-gramme and after a lot of hard slog in the studio, she brought out her debut single, 'Maybe That's What It Takes' – a song she premiered on the final and won plaudits from the panel and audience at the time – which reached number three in the UK charts.

A week later and just a fortnight after winning the show, contin-uing with her buzzy whirlwind of releases and striking the *Fame Academy* iron while it was still hot, her first album, *Introduction*, came out and got to number five in the album charts, shifting 500,000 copies. Seven of the songs were at least partially penned by Alex and one, 'Not Your Average Kind Of Girl', was written by her *Fame Academy* pals Carolynne Good and James Fox.

Even with the 500,000 copies of the aptly named *Introduction* – which also carried covers of Annie Lennox, Coldplay, Christina Aguilera and R.E.M. songs – sold, double platinum status in the UK, gold status in six European countries, Alex followed the pattern of TV talent show contestants, reaping the rewards from being on the box as soon as the show had ended.

However, unlike many fellow winners, who are often pictured tripping in and out of VIP-packed parties, arms laden with bags of freebies and new best friends clinging to their arms, Alex was not a fan of the pop star lifestyle as portrayed by the tabloids. Asked about the lavish gifts bestowed upon her, she showed what could almost be termed annoyance. Celebrity, her? Concerned with fame, her? Like the gifts, her? No, no, no.

Instead she appeared reluctant to accept the enviable house, zippy car and champagne lifestyle and said that though she was grateful to the BBC for giving her music a showcase and putting her 'out there', which is what she had initially wanted from the programme, she was not happy with the BBC's assumption that they could control her career outside of the TV studios just because she'd won the show or that the presents really mattered to her.

"All I wanted from *Fame Academy* was a launch into the music industry," Alex told *The Mirror*. "I couldn't give a toss about the flat and the car. Or the champagne, which is still in the fridge. I hate the stuff. They [BBC] helped but they did not ultimately put me where I am and they do not have ownership of me."

So the new *Fame Academy* winner cracked on with working on her music to prove that she was more than just a face from the telly who would nod and smile and accept champagne in return for a few well-placed compliments about her time on the programme. She just wouldn't do that.

Alex took 18 months off from the charts to work on her second album, *Honesty*, the title sending the message that she was back and this time she was her absolute genuine self. It came out in 2005 and reached number 24 in the charts, hinting that the Cornish singer had a steady base of fans. It also received glowing reviews for her new folk-ish sound, unlike its predecessor, which relied heavily on covers. "I already had enough of my own songs, but it would have been a crap album," Alex told BBC. "I needed a transition. The next one will be all original songs."

On Alex's official MySpace page, fans vented their fury when Polydor, Alex's label, released her lead single, 'Honesty', online rather than give it a release in the shops. Later in 2006, Alex and Polydor parted company and she went to Australia to work on improving her songwriting skills. During interviews she said she'd been trying to steer herself away from *Fame Academy* and any negative connotations the show might bring. It was pretty unusual for a TV talent show winner to make crotchety comments about the show that launched her so soon after their win.

"To be honest I feel stigmatised by *Fame Academy*," she told the *Daily Mirror* in 2003. "Being associated with it is a hurdle and not a help. I am working to get rid of it."

Nick Hall, who was on the same series as Alex, intimated something similar, that he'd found that having been on the BBC show was seen as a blight on his career by some sectors of the music industry. While Alex had already signed a contract with a record label, he found it a hindrance when he tried to get a recording deal. Evidently, the association with the programme deterred potential labels from signing him.

"The *Fame Academy* millstone was a distinct problem for me when it came to trying to get a record deal," he says. "In late 2007, I toured a little around the UK, supporting other up and coming artists and playing venues like the IndigO2, Canary Wharf, the Regal Room in London – I had a short residency at Tony Moore's place at the Regal Room, which became my second home for a little while – and towards the end of this period we – my manager and publisher and me – started to play a few showcases for major labels.

"We got pretty close to a deal with one of the majors who came to see me a few times, but in the end my back story just didn't add up to a good financial proposition from a record label perspective."

Unfortunately for Nick, he found that sum total of his life was whittled down to having been a *Fame Academy* contestant. The label needed a hook to pin on him to package him to fans and the press and they felt that his personal attributes and talent would be over-shadowed by his having appeared on *Fame Academy*. As such, people might judge him unfairly for already having his chance in the pro-gramme. Another concern was that having appeared on *Fame Academy*, the public might feel they knew all there was to know about him simply because they've seen them on the show.

"Labels need a story nowadays to promote and sell an artist," says Nick, "and the A&R guy reckoned he'd need about £2million to break me and didn't think I had enough of a story to 'sell' to his shareholders. At the time, James Blunt was coming out and had a perfect story to launch himself – an army officer having a major career move to singing.

"All I had as my back story was *Fame Academy* and it was always going to be difficult to sell me as 'that bloke who once did that *Fame Academy* thing'. Even if I had slept with someone famous, or lost a limb I'd still have been called 'the one from *Fame Academy*' so the major record deal never came, and eventually the publishing deal ran out. With no record deal to hang it off, there was little the publisher could do other than keep pitching my songs to other artists.

"During the latter stages of this whole thing, my manager and mentor passed away suddenly from a cancer treatment-induced stroke, which was a massive blow both to my music career and personally. So I put music on hold for a while and have concentrated on my family for a couple of years."

Nick's story highlights how hard it can be for contestants who finish lower down in the ranking, come off the show with some kind of profile but without the benefits of the management and recording deals that are divvied up among those who stay in the programme until the end. Even if some of those find that their deals are short-lived, they do at least get to 'realise their dream' of releasing an album.

As such, it's easy to see why Alex's peers might think she should have seized the opportunity presented to her because they don't arise that often – as many of them have found out. Gary Phelan agrees that those who last the length of the show get more support than contestants who bow out before the halfway point of the series.

Gary thinks that Alex should have made more of her chance to work with the major label instead of jacking it all. After all, she did say she wanted to focus on her music and when she was given a chance to do just that, she still seemed irked by the way in which she'd come to the attention of the label. "The winners of *Fame Academy* got all the best back-up from the show and had a great shot at succeeding," says Gary. "Everyone who stayed in the show longer than I did was signed to the same management and will have had lots of support from the people around them who have plenty of experience."

Although Gary wasn't under the same management as the winner, the upside to this was that he'd had more time and attention lavished on him than would be the case if he'd been signed to the same label as the rest of the series two rabble. "Because I came ninth, I was signed to a different label and management. Not the cheapest but not the same as theirs, which helps in a way because they have a bit more time for you and you're not competing with all those other people. The label is going to spend the most time on those who finished first and the others will probably have to take a back seat for a while, that's just how it goes and it's understandable given that the winner is supposed to have the big prize and the biggest career out of it.

"You know it's a competition and you know whoever finishes first will have the most money spent on them and that is fair enough but some of the contestants can become a bit lost because there are so many of them on the same label with pretty much the same story. But all the contestants signed to that management would have been given a good chance to make it.

"I think with Alex she didn't really grab the opportunity by the scruff of the neck. She did have the chance to do that and they had all the interest on her to make her something really big. Maybe in her own way she did but I think she should have gone for it a bit more and, if she had, I think she would still be in the charts now. She had the talent and she was liked enough to win but I don't know if she wanted to make it all that much and I'm not sure what she wanted from the show.

"I don't think she wanted the fame and the career in the charts and if she didn't then she did the right thing for her by getting out of it all but at the same time, if you go on *Fame Academy* then you'd think you'd be interested in having a degree of those things and you'd know that by going on TV there would be an element of that.

"You look at someone like Will Young. He really wanted it, he wanted to make it and be a popular singer and that was apparent on *Pop Idol*. He knew what he wanted and went for it. He threw himself into his career afterwards and he's still around today because he works at it and makes good decisions about his career."

Gary, who's still glad he went on *Fame Academy* for the opportunities it afforded him afterwards, thinks that the key distinction between a winner like Will Young and one like Alex Parks is that while Alex seemed to have a genuine love of singing and certainly had a talent for it, Will was more determined to succeed.

He accepted the quirks of fame and seemingly takes it as part of the job and always seemed to have a definite direction. Alex, however, had her talent and her likability but, for Gary, she never seemed to be sure whether it was for her or not. There are no ummers and ahhers in the music industry; you're either in and want to be in or you're out and, well, you want to be in.

"Maybe that's the difference in success and sort of disappearing from music and turning away from it all and being disheartened," says Gary. "It's the difference between really wanting to make it and having always wanted to make it and striving to get to a point that you're happy with and just going along with what is laid out in front of you with your heart not in it, and then leaving it all because it's not what you thought it would be.

"She's sort of turned her back on it all and distanced herself from the music she brought out and from the programme, but in doing that, she seems to have altogether given up on music. It's a shame in a way because she could have made something bigger of it all."

Alex's peer James Fox says that when he was on the show, he was wary of winning because he saw the winner's title could bring a lot of pressure but not much choice. When he applied, James knew that he wanted to paddle his own musical canoe and leave the *Fame Academy* race before he got so involved that too much was expected of him afterwards.

In this way, he thinks that Alex wasn't perhaps as wised up to the expectations that would be placed on her – by the BBC, by the record label, by fans and by the press – after winning the show and she reacted against it by going off and doing her own thing shortly after her win.

"I never wanted to win the show," says James. "I know that sounds crazy because why do you enter the competition if you don't want to win it? And it probably sounds silly me saying it because I didn't win, but I saw winning *Fame Academy* as like being handed a poisoned chalice.

"You go in and win these things and then you're very much the property of the BBC and whether you go away and do an album or whatever, they're controlling you because you have won their show and that's part of it. I never wanted that. It's a massive thing to be involved in but I know myself that there's another show next year, new contestants coming through and your shelf life is probably pretty short.

"It's an over-saturated market, the one the winners find themselves in, and if you've won you're going to be hot property and will be in every paper, TV show, radio show going, so people are sick to death of you after six months. Then you get your first album and tour and if it doesn't take off in a massive way, that's it. It's so much pressure and so much money is invested in the winner that you have to justify that that money has been well spent.

"They don't want you to plod along and have a career and work out what you want to do. They want a lot more from you than that and for whoever wins and however talented they are, it's a big ask of you but, understandably, the record label have to make back the time and money spent on you."

For all the time and money spent, James thinks that the winners' music and grand plans matter little unless it is selling, and if it isn't the people around the winner will move on to someone else who will shift more copies of their album. Contestants who don't finish first have more freedom away from these restrictions because they don't have the same level of hype and money plunged into them and aren't expected to do that well.

"I don't necessarily think those people at the label that they put you with care that much about your career," said James. "They'll drop you if you're not doing well. Without sounding too harsh on them, they want the next biggest thing; that's how the music industry works. If you're not that then they're not going to devote their time and money to you.

"These people are your new friends and family one minute but the next they drop you to make way for the next person and that's just the way things are, especially with the overcrowded TV contestants market. There's always someone new and more exciting coming out of a TV show.

"The winners are the biggest victims of that. The first album you get everyone cares about and wants to work on it. But if that doesn't do well enough then you won't get the songs for the second album to make you a success. The writers will want to work with the next best thing and that is often next year's winner. They won't want to linger around with a winner who hasn't done as well as expected if they can work with someone who might be more successful, especially if they're more receptive to the songs and direction the label wants to take them in."

As well as being uncertain over the way her career was shaping, James thinks that Alex Parks might not have had sufficient experience to deal with the change from being at college one minute to performing in front of millions the next, and that this might have stalled her ambitions. Besides which, he thinks it's unrealistic to expect someone with little background in music to sustain a career in the industry after only a few months of singing on the telly.

"Alex was at clown college before she went on the show," says James. "I'm not knocking her, I like Alex but to think that she could go on to have a 20-year music career coming straight out of clown college after going on to win the show in a matter of months, it's a bit naive on the parts of Polydor and the BBC.

"They might have 'found' her on the show but then they haven't got the writers to work with her because they've gone off to the next thing. And they couldn't go on and tell Alex what she should sing and in which direction she should go in because she didn't know, so she ended up doing things that weren't quite right. It was never going to work.

"Then it becomes a catch-22 situation because then the winner isn't happy with the next song and they're not in control of their own destiny and don't know where they want to go, so they can't change it and they end up putting out a single that no one is happy with and that people don't buy, so it all collapses for them."

James believes there was little scope for the winner to make mistakes and pootle along until the next good song came their way because by that point the interest in them would have died down altogether and they'll be seen as a failure for not sustaining early success.

This – the Steve Brookstein syndrome – occurs when the winner ends up playing smaller gigs and releasing new tracks that get lower placings in the charts than their earlier songs and so they are then written off as failures. Often, magnificent debuts are hard to recapture without the same level of interest and investment, and there can be a tendency after all that overexposure for people to expect the winner to fall, especially as they've seen previous winners fade away too.

As such, James is glad he stayed out of the top three in *Fame Academy* and got out in time to assert his career on his own terms without too much pressure being lumped on him. The pressure makes it hard for the contestant to succeed unless they have a clear focus of where they actually want to take their career. "You're only as good as your last song," he says. "People will remember that song and it's inevitable that you fail if you don't have the right songwriters or that amount of money reinvested into you or if people have tired of you by that point.

"That will be the song that stays with them until you bring out something else of any note, and if you keep bringing out songs that you're not happy with then they're going to lose interest in you anyway and associate you with songs that haven't done as well as your debut single and album. Or you get really lucky and go on to have big sales, a big band, a big tour and then, after a while, have a big crash. Then you end up with a big fat nothing because you won't be able to recapture that, and anything else on a smaller scale is seen as a failure.

"I can't say this for myself but anything other than prime-time television for these people is seen as a failure. If they pick up a guitar and play in a working men's club – as they might have done six months before their win – people will think they are failures. They're no better than they were six months ago and they deserve it almost. Which is ridiculous, there's nothing wrong with playing the working men's club circuit.

"And then people will say they expected that – that you'd fail anyway and you'd be back to playing the working men's circuit – even if you wanted to play at a working men's club anyway, so you can't win with them. I feel for them because they can't get around that, and it's hard for them to shake the tag of the TV show, winning it and then going on to do other things that don't fit in with winning; playing small venues and not having Top 5 albums.

"Whereas if you finish below the winner, you never have that weight of expectation and that feeling that you've failed if you're not on every chat show or doing world tours because it was never expected of you anyway, so you're free to shape your own career to suit you.

"That's why I wanted to get out before the last two contestants and certainly before the winner because I didn't want that. I knew it wasn't for me but I wanted to help myself along and give my career a boost so I went on the show. It started me off and I am grateful for that because at that time it didn't seem like there was any other way of getting out there but once I left, I made sure I could go down my own path without anyone telling me what to do or without me having to fulfil any obligations.

"They have it all planned for the winner [but] I had an idea of what I wanted and could get on with doing it in my own time."

While James had a clear plan in mind and wanted to get away from the show, Alex seemed a little more uncertain of what she wanted, even if she did know what she didn't want. Even so, BBC Chart Blog writer Fraser McAlpine thinks Alex's apparent dislike of the pop lifestyle and subsequent vanishing from mainstream music wasn't surprising, given that she might have lost respect from fans of the music she wanted to perform by relying solely on the TV show and their model of pop to sustain her career.

Despite having a loyal fan base, dismissing the programme altogether throws a whopping great spanner into the works because if you go on a TV show wanting to be a pop star and get your wish granted, it seems ungrateful to complain about it to those viewers who'd voted for you.

"Alex Parks is similar to Steve Brookstein from *The X Factor* in some ways," says Fraser McAlpine. "She won *Fame Academy* and then decided she didn't like the way things were shaping up for her and so she went off, did it all her own way and criticised the show when she was asked about it. She could have had all the attention available after winning but she rejected all of that. Her career isn't covered any more and maybe that's how she likes things.

"Fans of her music might have respected her for that. After all, she never professed any great need to be fronting any government schemes or promoting fizzy drinks on the release of her album, and they might still follow her music now but, on the flipside, she seems to have vanished completely. She's sort of become lumped into the group of winners from these shows that you never hear about any more, who just faded into the distance.

"It's a shame because she was unlike many of the performers you see on these TV shows. She had a really interesting voice and didn't just do karaoke covers. She was a very refreshing winner and the public warmed to that and I think having acts like Alex in shows like *Fame Academy* makes the whole thing more credible and more representative. People don't just buy singles and albums from 18-year-olds singing covers.

"So as a fan you might be thinking, well what was the point of her appearing on the programme anyway if she never wanted to be part of that scene? Turning her back on it does look unappreciative from their perspective because they invested time and votes in her. She'd have seen what happened to David Sneddon the year before her, so she would have had some prior warning of what type of direction her career would be going in after the show.

"I do have sympathy with her if it wasn't all it's cracked up to be and she decided to get away from all that and find something that suited her better, but if I was a fan I'd be thinking why did you bother to go on *Fame Academy* if you didn't want to be a pop star? There were people on that show who did want that life and in some ways it looks unfair that they didn't get to win if she didn't want that anyway."

For Nick Hall, Alex's main problem was that she took too long to relaunch herself after her debut album and focused too much on being seen as someone with integrity who wrote her own songs rather than finding some well-written tunes penned by another songwriter. Conversely, by shunning her *Fame Academy* achievements, Alex did herself a disservice with record labels early on in her career, especially as she appeared to have all of the elements to ensure a long career.

"I think it's possibile to gain a good grounding in the music industry and sustain a career after winning a TV talent show but all the right puzzle pieces have to fall into place at the same time for it to happen," says Nick. "The show gives you an audience but if you don't have the right back story, image, songs, attitude you don't stand a chance. The trouble is that no one can tell you what any of those things look like, because they don't know that either, and that's the problem.

"It [star quality] is not something you can put your finger on, and the show cannot help you do it and they can't help you find it if it isn't there. Even if you have all those things in your favour, it can all be easily destroyed by the wrong 'plan' once you leave the show.

"Simon Cowell is extremely clever at getting it right with the *X Factor* finalists, picking the right style, songs and marketing avenues so that they have some success after the show.

"Alex Parks and David Sneddon's careers were terminal as soon as the record companies got hold of them and they didn't play on the success of the programme to push them."

As well as this, Nick reckons that too many contestants try to do too much at once rather than focusing on one aspect of their careers. Historically with *Fame Academy* winners, this has been to polish their songwriting skills, but Nick thinks they would have been wiser to concentrate on their singing voices. After all, they have decades stretched out in front of them to record their dub-step album.

"The biggest mistake a winner of one of these programmes can make is to aim for a 'credible' career as a songwriting artist straight after leaving the show," he says. "Alex Parks had all the right attitude, image and story but Polydor tried to make her into a 'credible' artist. They sent her off to America where she wrote a bunch of songs with Diane Warren and other people, and it took over a year to get an album together by which point they'd missed the boat by a long way.

"They should have just got some great angsty pop hits written for her and pushed her straight away. If you look at JLS, Alexandra Burke and Leona Lewis from *The X Factor*, they've all put out hit songs almost within six to nine months of leaving the show and had success with them. All of their songs are perfect pop hits and suit them and their story without trying to be 'credible'.

"So I think it works, as long as the recipe is perfect; right artist, right songs, and right plan to make them successful. Winning the show alone is not enough."

Seemingly, winning wasn't enough for Alex Parks – or at least the accessories that came with winning weren't up her street – and she took herself off soon after the release of her second album. Little has been heard of her career since. Unlike David Sneddon who realised that he wanted to be behind the scenes writing songs, Alex thus far seems not to have found her niche.

"If you are going to turn away from the lifestyle bestowed upon you after winning a TV show then it is better to accept that than to moan about it in every media outlet going," said Fraser McAlpine. "It probably won't do you any favours with fans so you'd be just as wise working on distancing yourself from the show and working on your music if you still wanted to pursue it, that is. The more you moan, the more you alienate people and they'll move on and find another singer who does what you do but doesn't bang on about it at every opportunity."

Quite. So with Alex stepping away from the long shadow cast by *Fame Academy*, what did the students from her year make of their ascent to fame? It seems they didn't think too highly of it. Nick Hall said that a few months after leaving the show, he found that the sooner he dropped any associations with it the better.

After one too many unwelcome showbiz bashes mingling with people he didn't know, Nick realised that in order to succeed he needed to get his nose back to the grindstone and away from the fame that the show had afforded him. "You have a very short period

– in my case about three months before I got sick of it – of 'pretending' to be famous," says Nick.

Nick found himself with two or three invites to film premieres, the odd showbiz party, and the opportunity to 'jump the queue' at popular London nightclubs – even ahead of some 'real' celebs from the likes of *Corrie* and *Hollyoaks*, which earned him plenty of disapproving looks. "In my case, I didn't enter the show out of some desire for fame or fortune, I just wanted to sing and write songs, so 'networking' with people I didn't really know or care about in overpriced clubs didn't float my boat."

When Nick was asked to perform at gigs, he found that the types of music event he was asked to play weren't as beneficial as he'd hoped. Yet again the songs he'd been given to sing on the programme were overshadowing the work he was getting in the show's immediate aftermath. "You do get the odd gig out of the management company but mostly charity-type arrangements where someone wants a couple of *Fame Academy* rejects to open a fundraising event or such like," he says. "While doing these events is all very worthwhile and rewarding, it doesn't kick-start the career you've been hoping for – particularly when you're having to sing the cover songs you had thrust upon you by the show's producers and not your own music. Once you've got over the first three months after leaving *Fame Academy,* reality sets in and you realise that if you do want to follow a career in the music industry, the path you've just taken is likely to put more barriers in your way than open doors."

James Fox thinks that too many contestants get lured into doing shows like *Fame Academy* because they want to brush past the stars of *Hollyoaks* on their way to a life of starry parties and supermarket openings. He feels there needs to be more emphasis on contestants who really have unique talent or who are competing because they love music.

"I'm a musician first and foremost and that's why I went on *Fame Academy*; to help my career in music," says James. "The line between celebrity and music has become blurred on these programmes and the reasons why people enter them seem to have shifted from pursuing music to pursuing celebrity.

"I never wanted to become a celebrity and although some degree of that comes with that for some singers, I've been busy working in music, that's what I've always wanted to do but for some people the only reason they entered was because they want to be on the BBC, on the programme and in the papers.

"People said to me at the time, 'Oh it must be great being on the TV and in the papers every week'. That's the misconception people have when you go on one of these shows. I just wanted to play music, which is what I've been doing solidly all my life, being on TV just came with it for a while.

"There are peaks and troughs and moments where I've been more successful than others in my music but I'm on my own path you know and whatever happens, my ambition to play music hasn't changed, that's remained constant.

"Some of these people come from other jobs and haven't been doing music full time. They've got a good voice, they think they can sing on the show and their lives will change straight away. They're setting themselves up for a fall because it must be a disappointment when it all drops off, because then what are they left with?

"In the last 10 years celebrity has become the big thing caused in part by these shows and suddenly everyone wants to be in the limelight, everyone wants a piece of it and that's what some of these singers chase. If you asked everybody in that queue of 25,000 people for *Fame Academy* what they wanted, I'm not sure that most people would say they wanted to enter to sing and play music. They'd say they want people to know their names and be famous and for me, that's the wrong reason. The world's very driven by that, that *OK!* magazine culture.

"I know there are a lot of people who think being a songwriter or being a singer is the most important thing but I also know that a good percentage of people in that queue would also go along to the *Big Brother* auditions because they just want to be on these shows and get that slice of fame whatever it takes.

"Unless you're something special, you'll fade out because there's always another show around the corner and there are always people who can sing well enough and who will audition next year. It's not slowing down. I'm amazed that people still expect so much from the show, having seen what other people have gone on to and having seen how many contestants there are in the charts."

Worse still, James knows of some hopefuls, certain that the talent show would be their route to eternal fame and wealth, who packed in their jobs and old lives because they thought it would all change once they appeared on the telly every week. "I know a lot of people who have left their jobs or told their managers what to do with their jobs when they went on these shows, thinking that everything would change and that they wouldn't need to go back to their old lives," he says. "The show puts you at the start of the race and you've got to have a certain level of pedigree to get there but you have to do the rest. You can't just expect that level of fame, success and money just from being on the TV. But a lot of them did and I don't think it will ever give that level of success to everyone coming on to the show.

"People in my show had real jobs before entering *Fame Academy*. I had just assumed that everybody would have been a jobbing musician beforehand. Some of these people walk on these shows not really knowing what they want from it and then go in for the wrong reasons, for the fame and money, or they get completely thrown in at the deep end and then don't know what to do and panic.

"I feel sorry for a lot of friends I met on the show because they're so disillusioned with it all now. They thought their lives would change for going on the show and that it would mean that they'd have everything handed to them. But maybe in thinking that they were punching above their weight almost, because there are always new contestants and new programmes and interest dips in everyone after a while."

One of those whom James thinks took too much of a leap all at once was Alex. "You look at Alex Parks; one minute she's at clown college in Cornwall and the next she's on *Top Of The Pops*," he says. "There needs to be something in between all of that. Unless you have a really great voice, there has to be more than that.

"Leona Lewis has a great voice but essentially she was just a singer who went on one of these shows and has done well and who has gone on to become world class. But if you're just a good singer, well there are plenty of good singers, you'll come and go like everybody else. If you have that year or six months of people patting you on the back and massaging your ego then you take that opportunity because a lot of people won't get that.

"You have to see it as that rather than, 'It's not fair. My career's over, I should have had more than I was given'. People have got the wrong attitude. They give you the platform and the background and then you have to run with it. People expect so much just because they can sing but they should be a bit more grateful for what they almost had and move on from that. You can't expect people to care about you afterwards just because you've been on the TV. You've got to make things happen for yourself once you're off the TV every week."

Nick Hall was a contestant who took heart in his chance to move away from the *Fame Academy* side of his career. Once he was dropped by the management and label he was signed to after he left the show, rather than leaving him at a loose end, beating his fist on the floor and whining that life isn't fair, Nick felt happy to be freed from the restraints of the label and to be the big cheese in shaping his career. This meant getting back to basics, getting songs written and taking on some part-time work so that he could pay the bills in the meantime.

"The bottom six from the show all got dropped by the management company after six months, closely followed by the rest of the contenders," says Nick. "This was not unexpected and was a welcome freedom to pursue other avenues. For me this meant going back to the drawing board and working on writing some decent songs.

"One comment that stuck with me was that 'Success is all about the songs… if you were to write U2's "Beautiful Day" I'd probably be able to get you a deal tomorrow'. So for a good two and a half years after the show, this was what I focused on. I put my head down, worked part-time to pay the mortgage and got on with writing songs that I believed in, that I'd buy and that I'd listen to.

"It's very easy to get wrapped up in the 'business' side of stuff, trying to please people and trying to make songs that you think they might want to hear, when the reality is that if you don't write songs you're proud of, no one else is likely to be bothered about them either.

"One of the things David Grant said to me that stuck with me to this day was that you can write and sing to impress people and you might impress a few people, but if you write and sing with meaning, truth and emotion you will always impress people."

So Nick's work started to reap rewards and his *Fame Academy* days were largely pushed aside. In his quest to get his career started on his own terms, Nick shed his *Fame Academy* skin so much that most of those he worked with were oblivious to him having been a contestant.

"Eventually I wrote a couple of songs that paid off," he says. "In particular one song, 'Stronger', started to get a lot of plays on my MySpace page. A few people started to hear it in the industry and things started to happen.

"A freelance agent got me on stage supporting Bryan Adams at the opening of the RICOH Arena in Coventry, which was an amazing experience and also got a couple of music publishers interested. Eventually I signed a deal with a smaller independent publisher for the rights to my songs. I turned down a much bigger cheque from a major publisher as I believed the smaller publisher had a better plan. A publishing deal buys the rights to the songs – it's not a record deal so it doesn't get you selling records.

"This finally allowed me to stop working and focus on my music for a couple of years. I flew to Los Angeles to record some tracks with a producer out there and had some interesting musicians play on my songs – Iggy Pop's bass player, Kelly Clarkson's guitarist and a host of amazing musicians and gospel singers. I co-wrote a bunch of songs with some incredible songwriters – Greg Fitzgerald, Midge Ure, Ali Thomson to name a few – and ended up with a pretty strong couple of albums' worth of material. Through all of this, we – everyone involved – never really mentioned *Fame Academy*. Whenever it was mentioned, it was always seen as a step along the path I'd taken to get to this point, which in truth it was."

Despite moving himself away from the *Fame Academy* brand and becoming known as a chap who didn't need to rely on a TV programme to promote his songs, Nick still holds his head high when and if people mock shows like *Fame Academy* and dismiss him for going on it.

"I had some further success with my own digital release of 'Sticks And Stones', which was picked up by one of the anti-bullying charities and became the official song of Anti-Bullying Week in 2007," says Nick. "The song did reasonably well in the HMV download charts, peaking at number six between Kylie Minogue and Girls Aloud, which isn't such a bad place to be. The song has received airplay around the world and even been published in an English language educational CD/book in Germany.

"After *Fame Academy,* you stop getting recognised in the street pretty quickly. I occasionally get a sideways stare from people who are sure they recognise me from somewhere but can't quite put their finger on it. No one ever stops to ask though. I just smile quietly to myself knowing that I chased a dream and got within fingernails of making it stick. How many people in their lives can stand tall and proud and say that?"

Despite this, Nick understands that the type of profile that contestants are given on *Fame Academy* is transient and that it is understandable – and in many ways beneficial – that after a few months people forget the contestants who didn't finish in the top three or at least forget the genre of music they sang and the particulars of their musical ambition. This is something that he and other contestants have come to accept in the months after they've appeared on the programme. Similarly, Nick says he learned pretty quickly not to expect too much of the show because going on *Fame Academy* or *The X Factor* can only push you along so far.

"The show didn't help my career in any direct way," he says. "I did make a few good friends, and have a few fans from the show who've stuck by my career throughout, which I'm thankful for, but in general no one really remembers people who dropped out of these shows short of the last two or three.

"Usually when people do, they remember that you left early, not what you did, what you sang or whether you were actually any good or not. People watch these programmes as popcorn TV while they're eating food on a Saturday night.

No one really cares what happens to the people who win or lose as long as they enjoy their Saturday night viewing. I count myself as one of these viewers too."

As an ex-contestant Nick understands this more than most and has come to view talent TV programmes as simply light entertainment and nothing more than that. And that means that he no longer sees them as viable ways to leapfrog into the charts.

For Nick, contestants are just characters and even if that isn't apparent to hopefuls when they audition, it becomes crystal clear when they watch the playbacks on which they were presented as "the cute one who still gets his mum to do his laundry" or the "one who is a bit ditzy because she wears un-ironed clothes and tripped on one of the stairs to the stage".

In Nick's case, he protested against some of the decisions made for him, including the clothes he was given to wear. Since leaving the show, however, he understands that though he disliked the way he was styled and the songs he was handed to sing, it was just part of being on the TV show.

"After being on one of these shows, you soon understand the reality is that they are simply TV shows, not launch pads for musical ambitions. Once you understand that it is a TV show though, the decisions the producers make all start to make sense to you," says Nick. "Jedward from the sixth series of *The X Factor* are a case in point, pure genius from a TV producer's point of view.

"In *Fame Academy*, we had very little control over anything in the house, we had no choice on songs – these were dictated to us by committee – BBC producers, Endemol and Polydor – and even less choice about what we wore or how we were styled.

"I remember arguing bitterly about the nasty tie-dyed pink T-shirt they made me wear on my final night (especially as Alistair [Griffin] had been wearing it earlier in the day) and the shoes that were a size too big for me, but in the end I still had to wear them.

"The only real benefit from *Fame Academy* during this whole process was the appointed music lawyer who to this day still helps me and guides me. He is a good, honest chap who really loves music and always helps the little guys get a break wherever he can. If there's one thing I'm grateful to *Fame Academy* for, meeting him is it, it's just a shame that I've never earned enough money from it to pay him back."

Like a ghost ship approaching in the distance, the legacy of being a 'loser', that is not being the winner on a TV talent show, is something that still gets Nick's goat today. Sure, not winning might technically make you a loser but after being picked from thousands of other singers to get to that stage, its connotations are harsh.

Finishing outside of the top three, and not having the benefit of more time to display your winning personality and non-desperate nature, Nick has found that people may remember only that he was on the show and then see fit to judge him unfairly for doing so. The thing to take comfort in is that talent is often spurned in favour of good TV, says Nick, so while leaving the show may be unfortunate at the time, it doesn't necessarily signify who is the most or least talented.

"I think it's human nature to judge people based on what you've seen of them, rightly or wrongly," he says. "The problem is that by entering one of these shows you are putting yourself under the microscope and asking the world to find all your faults. It is our nature to criticise and point fingers at other people when they are different from ourselves, and reality TV shows allow us to do this in the comfort of our own homes without fear of retribution. It's almost a public service allowing us all to feel better about ourselves by laughing at the misfortune of others.

"So talent shows have to do both – find people the public will like, and others the public will laugh at – it's a double-edged sword between TV show and performance competition and in general the TV show wins out until towards the end of a run when the last few acts are left and it all turns serious.

"I know a good few people who stopped watching *The X Factor* in series six when Jedward stayed in over Lucie Jones, complaining that it was 'unfair'. I thought it was genius. The sheer volume of people debating the programme, the press, the hype… it all added to the programme.

"The only loser in the whole thing was Lucie, even though she was probably one of the most talented vocalists on the show – proof in point that it's all about the TV show and has little to do with finding a genuine artist. Simon Cowell wins regardless of which name ends up in the final box.

"People often make comments about how you got booted out, or how you lost or how you were a 'loser' but my response is always the same: what have you done to chase your dreams lately?

"I got further than most, and at least I tried. My favourite comment after I came out of the show was from a fairly famous musician friend who has played on stage at arena gigs around the world (and was among the headline acts at Live8) who told me that I had 'big brass balls to go on TV and subject myself to that level of intrusion' and that he 'couldn't have done it'."

One contestant who was reluctant to apply and allow in that level of intrusion was James Fox. James had been playing instruments and singing in bands for 12 years before he went on *Fame Academy*. He was keen to keep pursuing music but couldn't get a leg up in the industry and was advised to go on a talent show to get himself noticed.

Many of his musician friends mocked him for applying for the show and trying to move his career along that way but James thinks that at the turn of the century, with MySpace and band blogging yet to take off in a big way, shows like *Fame Academy* were among the only platforms where new singers could launch themselves.

"I never wanted to go on any of these shows and going on one was seen as selling out by all of my musician friends," says James. "They saw me going on *Fame Academy* as selling out rather than doing things the 'hard way', playing small gigs, working on songs and trying to get the interest of record labels.

"Well I'd been doing things 'the hard way' for 12/13 years and the industry wasn't opening up for me. At that time, if you weren't on one of these shows then you had no chance. So I saw the one that had the best foundations and that it was more of an academy that taught you about music more than just being a pop puppet for want of a better word, and doing a bit of karaoke every Saturday night and then becoming someone who could be manipulated after the show had ended."

Every time James went to talk to people about his music and doing things 'the hard way', they'd suggest giving one of the shows a whirl and after one too many people warned him that to get anywhere with music types you had to be between 18-24, he gave *Fame Academy* a shot before his youth slipped away.

"At the time of me applying for *Fame Academy* there had been *Popstars*, *Pop Idol* was on, and this was the second series of *Fame Academy*," he says. "It felt hard to get recognised without going on one of these shows. All of this started in the past decade and at the start of the century it felt that getting on in the industry was impossible unless you appeared on telly.

"I kept hearing about this '18-24' year-old bracket wherever I went to ask someone's advice about getting further and if you didn't make it then between those years then that would be it. Record companies kept saying that and the chance to do it and make it in the industry seemed to be getting smaller and smaller for me so I panicked really, so I just went for it. I thought I've got to get involved with this before it's too late because people kept saying to me, you need a TV show to launch yourself from, that's how you have to make it nowadays.

"To be honest at first I didn't want to go on *Fame Academy* and didn't want to get success that way and be known for doing things that way but then I thought I had to make a go of things so I did the show. I just saw it as doing what I'd been doing for years – singing and playing music – but just doing it to a bigger audience."

James believes the musical balance has now been readdressed with bands putting their music online and building up a fan base that way, and that it is possible to go on to have success without the backing and exposure of a TV programme. "The shows have sort of divided the industry and there's a bit more chance to make it without a show," he says. "The TV shows are still dominant but it's more healthy nowadays. People are now getting their music out there, on the internet, playing gigs without having to go on these TV shows. The Arctic Monkeys are the perfect example here.

"You'd never get them going on *The X Factor* but they've been helped in part by the growth of the internet and the way in which people now access music and hear about bands.

"The music industry is much more healthy now and there's a wider scope for bands and acts to break through but TV shows and the music contestants go on to record still makes up a huge part of the industry."

Even though James doesn't regret going on *Fame Academy*, like Gary Phelan and Nick Hall before him, he was also disappointed by the lack of real music instruction on the programme and wished they'd had more focus on honing their songwriting skills as they'd been promised. Instead, the show – though it gave his music a wider platform and has helped push him under the noses of the right people – was not dissimilar to the karaoke of *Pop Idol* and *Popstars*, which he'd been trying to avoid.

"I have no regrets about going on *Fame Academy* and it has helped my career but the content of it, I was disappointed with," says James. "We spent nine weeks in there with little time for music. I always think of it as like *Big Brother* with a weekly karaoke contest. We were promised so much at the start of the show, that there would be people like Sting and Elton John coming on to help us and mentor us with our singing and songwriting, but that didn't happen.

"Nobody came in to see us. It was made to sound like an academy of music where we'd have structured lessons on singing and songwriting every day but it really wasn't that. It was made out to be that but instead it was the karaoke show that we were promised it wouldn't be. It was a lot of sitting around twiddling our thumbs and not really knowing what to do with the time, it was really very poor. It was the human experiment that they promised us it wouldn't be and that I had hoped it wouldn't be. It had a real *Big Brother* element and I found that really disappointing because I never wanted to go on *Big Brother*, I just wanted to kick-start my music career."

Worst still, James says he didn't learn anything from doing the show and that the nine weeks sitting around not really knowing what to do had a detrimental effect on his creativity. The only thing James felt he learned from doing the show was how to best pose in front of the cameras. Still, the big draw of doing it and one that he still credits as helping to push his career along today was the peerless exposure that the prime-time TV show offered.

"I was just doing what I'd been doing for years but on a much larger scale. If anything I forgot things while I was in there rather than learn things because we were just sitting around so much doing nothing. Standing up and singing to a camera and knowing that millions of people were watching, that's something new I gained from it, and being on TV. It was a crash course in media training so that was something new to me, so I took that from being on the show.

"The thing that helped me was that I'd had loads of experience performing at gigs but the transition for some people was too much, there was no preparation. I might have played to considerably smaller crowds but I still knew what to do, but some people had had no experience of performance and then were thrust out there singing in front of all those millions of people.

"Without sounding like I knew it all before, you can't teach someone to look natural when they perform but for me it felt quite natural, it was just a bigger platform. Other people fell into that experience or took a lot more guidance. It was an extension of what I had in mind anyway and what I was doing from day to day because I was performing music full-time anyway and hadn't had another job or direction to distract me from working on my music."

James has pursued music consistently since the show and is happy with his varied career, which has been steered by him to suit his needs, but he found the image that people had of him when he left the show was hard to shake and was detrimental to him. "These shows create a hyper version of you and you might not be happy with that," he says. "You think you're going to get a fair hearing on these programmes and you're told you will do but you don't. They give you songs to sing, the clothes to wear and they mould you in a way that suits them. They know who they want to create you into even if that isn't really a fair representation of you.

"So when you come out of the show, you notice that people's perceptions of you are slightly distorted and they can think you're an altogether different type of artist or person because of how they've seen you on the programme. I wasn't happy with what was put across about me. I fought that a lot because I wasn't happy with it, which is why I didn't get along with so many people on the production side of the show."

However, one distinct bonus of going on *Fame Academy* was that there were plenty of meetings arranged with record labels that were more willing to talk to James and hear about his music after he left the programme. The only problem was that the association with a TV talent search meant that James was often swiftly dismissed because so many other contestants have faded into obscurity after a couple of months. "On the plus side, when you come out of *Fame Academy* the doors of production and management are opened up to you and there were a lot of meetings set up with record companies whereas before the doors were shut to me, so that was good," he says.

"A lot of the serious stuff... the *NME, Q,* and those types of music fans and executives would look down their noses at me for going on *Fame Academy* and I found I had to battle my way through that with people and prove that I wasn't just some kid who'd been on a TV show and didn't have any idea about music, and that I knew how to play instruments and that I'd done loads of things before going on *Fame Academy*. Going on it wasn't the sum of my life's work.

"There were a lot of barriers to knock down as a result of that. Then there was the problem of being tarred with the same brush as people who'd been on these shows and then had faded into obscurity. You've got to battle through this and prove that your music has merit and that you're different from all those other contestants.

"These shows do open so many doors for new singers and that's why you do it. You get these knock-backs and you do get written off early on but I saw more benefits as a way of getting into the industry than negatives."

Nick Hall also saw the benefits of bringing his music to a wider audience via *Fame Academy,* and enjoyed being part of the show in the first instance, but unlike some performers who repeatedly apply for these shows, he has no desire to apply to another TV talent search. "I often get asked 'Why don't you apply for *The X Factor?*'" he says. "My answer is always 'no'. I have no desire to be an insect under a microscope again, and even less to be a pawn in a TV show producer's game show. Don't get me wrong, at the time I enjoyed every second of it and the experience was all too short.

"The few months leading up to and on the show were a whirlwind of emotion and excitement both for me and everyone around me but there's no way I'd put any of my family and friends through it again."

One of the reasons that Nick, who has since supported Sporty Spice's singing bud Bryan Adams, wouldn't have another stab at it is because in his view, not enough was done to help him once he left *Fame Academy*. Once out of the *Academy's* mansion doors, he was treated very differently and didn't have as much counsel as he needed after such a huge experience.

Contestants were told that the show could change their lives but Nick reckons that the passage between being booted out of the

*Academy* and then going on to try to live a relatively normal life was far from smooth and that not enough helping hands were offered to make it a more seamless journey. "You have high hopes/expectations that 'things' will happen automatically when you enter a programme like *Fame Academy*," says Nick. "You are warned by producers about how hard the show is from a psychological point of view, but they do nothing to prepare you for the transition from being on the show to being back in the real world, other than a one or two-hour session with the psychologist immediately after you're kicked out to ensure you won't do anything stupid.

"However, you are then pretty unceremoniously booted out the door and after a night in a hotel, a brief appearance on CBBC the following day, you find yourself back home two days later wondering what the hell just happened?

"An example of just how unceremoniously you get booted out is that the BBC would not pay for a taxi home to Birmingham, all they would stump up for was train fare even though I had two suitcases, a guitar, a saxophone and a big box of random bits and pieces from my life they'd requested for use on BBC3/CBBC and only two hands to carry it all.

"But on a positive, you do leave the show with a 'real' manager, a lawyer and a very small contact book, which helps you get a foot in the door, but that's about it. Oh and some serious debts from not paying the mortgage for a couple of months."

Yet with a good deal of hindsight and greater knowledge of how the shows work than he had at the time, Nick reckons if he did get his chance over again he would have either stuck to his guns a bit more on the live finals so that he could demonstrate the type of music he wanted to play afterwards or he would have given headmaster Richard Park a bit more cheek.

"My goals before and while I was on the show were always and have always been to sing and write songs I'm proud of. This, I'm still doing. All the other stuff is really irrelevant and only gets in the way. Admittedly it would be nice to get the record deal and an outlet to get all my songs heard by a bigger audience, but right now I'm honestly happy doing what I'm doing, but could do with a bit more cash.

"If I'd known then what I know now, would I have still entered the show? Absolutely. I would change nothing about the audition process, but then I'm torn about how I'd deal with the live shows. I have two very different thoughts on it – I would either have ignored everything they told me to do, worn my own clothes, ignored all the TV side of stuff like which camera to look at, and how they told me to hold out my arms during particular words, basically all the stuff that's really irrelevant, and just got on with singing and made damn sure that I got the right song to sing on the night. I still wouldn't have been placed in the top six and I'd have probably been threatened with being dropped if I didn't play ball.

"I know a couple of the contestants on *The X Factor* who were 'difficult' and were forced to sing pretty embarrassing songs, which got them booted. Or I would have waited for the music to start, dropped my pants and mooned at Richard Park.

"I'd probably have had more success with my career if I'd have done the latter. I'm still waiting for the day when someone actually does it on the live portion of one of these shows. That will be a day to remember."

So there you have it. Future *X Factor* and TV talent show contestants you heard the man. Your route to success and shedding the label of being a 'loser' is to get Mary Whitehouse turning over in her grave and pull a moony.

# Chapter 5

# Pop Idol

Talking Will Young (weren't we?), for every argument based around the validity of TV searches for talent, he, along with Leona Lewis and Girls Aloud provide the answer that validates their worth. Even Sir Elton John, who in 2006 told *The Mirror* that he wasn't a fan of *The X Factor* and shows of its ilk, was quick to applaud Will Young for his singing. "Will Young is the best thing that's ever come out of those shows," said Elton. "He has proved himself."

With Sir Elton's blessing ringing true, Will has continued to stay ahead of the pop game long after his *X Factor* triumph and has certainly proved himself a commendable singer with an impressive back catalogue.

Will's career has been longer and more successful than most acts that launched themselves at the turn of the century – Les Ketchup and Scooter where are you now? Make yourselves known – and, indeed, he seems apart from the genre as a whole. It seems inconceivable that not so long ago Will, the first winner of *Pop Idol*, was seen by many as the underdog compared with his fellow finalist Gareth Gates, a Bradford teen with an angelic face, voice and triumphant back story – he stuttered in speech but not while singing.

Will didn't stutter. He sang and spoke with self-assurance gleaned through his studies at the Arts Educational School (previous alumni of the schools include Julie Andrews and Michaela Strachan) in Chiswick in West London, which specialises in music, drama and dance.

At the grand young age of 23, he had more experience of the big, wide world than his nearest rival Gareth Gates. With the tamed (no more Britney Spears impressions and bold assertions) and charming Darius Danesh out of the race, it was left to Will and Gareth to win over the final voters to be crowned our next great *Pop Idol*.

It was a closely fought battle in which both he and Gareth, showing plenty of camaraderie towards one another, were propped up on the sofas with Lorraine Kelly in an election-style campaign to drum up support before the final showdown. That meant riding around the country in tour buses with their names emblazoned on the sides and going back to their home towns to josh around with teary-eyed locals who regaled stories of when the lads sang Rogers & Hammerstein numbers at the church fete. The two chaps wore sharp suits and rosettes with their names on and pledged to be worthy ministers of pop should they be afforded that chance.

So it was that two trilling chaps were pounding the streets meeting their pop constituents, defining their pop policy, being on hand to answer any wavering doubts and telling the people that the famous panel were actually really nice and surprisingly, much smaller in real life – would you believe? – and pretty much earning their votes.

On the final night and with 53.1% of the vote (4.6 million of the 8.7 million votes cast), Will took the first year's winner's title on the much-hyped ITV1 show where he – and Gareth – put his spin on the winner's single 'Anything Is Possible' to the crowd and the viewers.

Since leaving the show, Will has shifted eight million copies of his albums and his debut song, 'Anything Is Possible/Evergreen' – the song bestowed on him as winner of the show and, incidentally, a track featured on Westlife's album *World Of Our Own* – is the fastest-selling debut in UK chart history, beating Hear'Say's record, attained earlier that year, with 'Pure And Simple'. Three weeks later he was knocked off the number one spot by Gareth Gates' cover of the pop standard 'Unchained Melody', a song he'd sung on the show and that is reportedly among Simon Cowell's favourite tracks.

Incidentally, Will's debut, 'Evergreen', and Gareth's cover are the top two best-selling hits of the Noughties, outselling Kylie Minogue, Robbie Williams, Britney Spears and yes, even Shaggy who got to number three with 'It Wasn't Me' in 2000. Their success is testament to the early boom of the TV talent search and enabled Will to lay down the foundations for his impressive music career.

Coming reality/talent TV full circle, Will also went on the fourth series of *The X Factor* where he helped Cheryl Cole pick her finalists, mentored nervy contestants, praised young Blackburn singer Diana Vickers for her unusual style (for a TV talent contest) and performed his single 'Grace' on the show. He even got mixed up in a bit of controversy, telling reporters that he wasn't entirely convinced that the contestants were singing live on their group performances afterwards.

Will has since had a bit part in teen drama series *Skins* as a Michael Jackson-mad teacher and appeared in Brit-flick *Mrs Henderson Presents* with Dame Judi Dench. Intuitively enough, he even had intuitions about doing so. "I had premonitions about winning a talent contest and appearing in a film with Judi Dench – and then both came true," Will told the *Daily Mail*. Spooky.

For BBC Chart Blog writer Fraser McAlpine, Will's success can be attributed not to his unnerving pop premonitions, but in part to his distancing himself from the *Pop Idol* and reality TV brand early on in his career, rather than trading on it at every opportunity like Hear'Say before him. By doing so, Will gave his music a chance to be judged on its quality rather than how it came to prominence.

"Will Young is the first winner who seemed to dissociate himself from what the show and shows like it had been like," said Fraser. "The perception of what it meant to be a contestant and a winner changed when he went on *Pop Idol* and has been followed by contestants who've also gone on to become successful and sustain a career in their own right, like Girls Aloud.

"As soon as he went on *Pop Idol,* Will Young marked himself out as someone different from what we'd seen before on these shows because he was prepared to stand up for himself and argue with Simon Cowell.

"Will Young was ornery. He knew what he wanted out of the programme and what sort of career he wanted afterwards and he didn't back down. He may have accepted their comments but you were left with the impression that he had a clear idea of how he wanted things to shape out. No one had done that before, challenging the judges' authority in a polite way that earned him the respect of viewers and didn't come across as ridiculous.

"When you look back at the show, what he really said was tame and he remained pretty polite compared with the backchat nowadays, the way in which many contestants retaliate to any comments made about their performances, but at the time it was refreshing and made for good television.

"It set him apart from the other contestants and, in doing so, gave him something different to start his career with, it gave him a new story almost. It made him seem more credible almost."

Mr Holy Moly, the anonymous voice of one of the UK's favourite gossip websites holymoly.co.uk., thinks that Will's success can be attributed in part to his detachment from *Pop Idol.* "Will Young managed to pull himself away from *Pop Idol* and spent quite a lot of time working on his songs," he says. "He was never going to sell out Wembley Stadium on a Saturday evening and have a U2-style album straight away but what he and his management did do was to work out the best way of getting the longest career possible out of him. They made a lot of savvy moves.

"A lot of that is down to songs. If your first single out of *Pop Idol* or *The X Factor* is going to be some shitty cover version and you do more shitty cover versions after that you can't expect to have any longevity whereas if you get back and work on a song like Will Young did with 'Leave Right Now' you can see why it works.

"At the beginning of these shows it was very much about chucking out any old shit with people like Gareth Gates and the early contestants. But on the flipside they can leave it too long. Leona Lewis won *The X Factor* in 2006 and she still hasn't done a tour. There needs to be a balance and a degree of savviness."

Once Will had left *Pop Idol* and set to work on his career, Fraser thinks that his disaffiliation with the show – soon after he brought out his winner's single and a cover of 'The Long And Winding Road' with Gareth Gates – helped him become acknowledged among fans and critics and become accepted for his singing talent and not because of the programme that launched him.

"When Will left the show, he did the typical winner's single that every contestant does and that is expected of them," said Fraser. "It by definition is pretty generic so that it can suit any one of the finalists and so doesn't really show off their style.

"More, it is a representation of the show and its power that it can get to number one at the biggest single week of the year – Christmas. Unlike most winners, Will's wasn't released for the Christmas single market but it was as you'd expect for a first single from a winner of one of these shows. If you're only given a week to record it and make the video, then what can you expect?

"He then did a Beatles cover with Gareth Gates and that was pretty much the extent of his *Pop Idol* career or his career along the lines of other winners from these TV shows. But he very quickly moved over and away from *Pop Idol* and into doing things that were very much in his style, in his interest and recorded music that isn't usually divvied up among contestants.

"He didn't just do cover after cover or push any old thing for the sake of it. He might have released music soon after he won the show, but there seemed to have been a lot of thought into what sort of artist he was and what his fans would like to listen to. That's the difference.

"All of this moved him away from the TV show and made him an artist in his own right. That he's quite opinionated also probably helped this because you don't get him just nodding and going along with things in interviews. He will speak his mind and this keeps fans and the press interested in him. He's had a bit of a life outside of what usual winners go on to do, *Pop Idol* is a part of that but it's not the sum of his life and it's not the only point of conversation with him.

"The lesson is that if the TV programme that you were launched on is the only thing that people are interested in about you, then your career as a chart artist probably won't be that long," says Fraser.

"There will always be another show, another winner and someone else with the same story as you – that you won a TV show or that you sang on a TV show – if that is all you're relying on to win people over with. Although that can get you to a certain point of success, having something else about you and moving away from the show you first appeared on seems to help enormously with sustaining it and becoming respected among your fans and critics.

"The songs Will Young has recorded are contemporary and are very different from the type of songs you imagine a male winner to go on to release, especially as the male winners tend to stall after a few covers and nods to Justin Timberlake or Michael Bublé. In fact, as with all contestants who've gone on to better things, it seems strange to even imagine him going on that show singing covers and waiting for the judges' comments."

As well as having songs that matter and becoming known for his music and not the famous TV programme he once appeared on, along with a gaggle of other people, Fraser thinks that Will's determination to make his career in his own image has helped separate him from the heaps of other reality TV winners and contestants that have come along after him.

"He made his career his own and has gone on to become such a success because he's had a steer in it and that steer has been away from *Pop Idol* and what reality shows traditionally do," said Fraser. "He's got to the stage now where he has a loyal fan base and he can labour over his albums a little longer and experiment with them.

"He can go off to the West End or make a film and his fans are still going to be there to buy his next album. A lot of the contestants struggle to be remembered after a couple of months but he has remained distinctive and that makes all the difference."

So Will Young has had the level of success in his career befitting of the title *Pop Idol*. Even the pop prince Gareth Gates has done pretty well for himself, having found acclaim for his roles in West End productions and having sold 3.5 million records in the UK (despite being dropped in 2006 and last releasing a single with his new label in 2008).

Gareth, who's now father to a daughter, even had a brief relationship with pin-up Jordan aka Katie Price, which ensured him of a few tabloid headlines. Nowadays, Gareth is loved up with his partner, Suzanne, whom he met at a Record of the Year bash where he was up for an award for his cover of 'Unchained Melody'. Despite the success that Gareth has achieved, Fraser thinks that if he had won he wouldn't have gone on to have the commendation that Will has now.

"If Gareth Gates had won, it would have been a different story," says Fraser. "He was a teenager when he went on the show but Will had come out of university and had a bit more of an idea of how he wanted things to play out.

Gareth's voice was very boy-band-ish, as were his styling and his influences. He adored Westlife who were pretty stale by the time he went on *Pop Idol*. Gareth's career would have been the ballads, the covers of ballads and nice white suits and all the things he did once he left the show anyway and that eventually people stopped buying into.

"There's nothing wrong with that type of pop but after doing one album like that, it doesn't really entice fans into buying your next album because they know it'll be more of the same and they could get that from Westlife anyway. He would have been dropped after a year because that type of music isn't what most pop fans want because there's plenty of that around already, even if they did like him and initially vote for him."

Luckily, Gareth, who at the height of his fame had a cameo in the S Club 7 film *Seeing Double*, has gone on to success in the West End and plays Marius in the International 25th Anniversary World Tour production of *Les Miserables*. In true reality TV tradition, he even popped up on celebrity skate-off *Dancing On Ice* where he finished in fourth place, with former Hear'Say singer Suzanne Shaw taking the winner's medal. Let's hope the next time Gareth appears on a reality-cum-celebrity-competition show he'll be crowned the winner. Third time lucky and all.

While Gareth is off lighting up the West End with his hammed-up roles, third place *Pop Idol* Darius Danesh is treading the reality TV boards again in *Popstar to Operastar* on his channel home ITV. The reality TV competition umbilical cord is always there to cling on to and rejoice in if nothing else pops up.

Meanwhile, Will Young has been busy crafting the sort of decisions that have kept him in the pop game long after he could have dropped out or fallen by the wayside. In fact, his clever decisions have earned him the respect of his pop peers.

Tony Lundon, who was a member of Liberty X, also thinks that Will's success can be attributed to the strength of mind and determination that he and his team showed in performing songs that worked for him very early on in his career and putting his label's nose out of joint by bringing out a 'difficult' second album featuring a beat poetry bonus CD and a duet with Bob the Builder. This direction was smartly thought out and executed by all around him.

"I think with Will Young's career, a lot of the success can be credited to intelligent decision making," says Tony. "Every single, every video, producer, agent, every enemy or ally you make has an effect on your career. Will and his team seem to me to be able to make good decisions for themselves without alienating the label so everyone's happy, everyone has ownership. But that's just an outsider's guess."

So while Will, a politics graduate, went on to see his premonitions come true and his music appreciated throughout the music community – he even had an hour-long *South Bank Show* about him to cement his achievements – his *Pop Idol* successor wouldn't go on to follow in his magnitude and longevity. Or at least, she hasn't so far.

She was Michelle McManus who was 23 – the same age as Will when he won the programme – at the time she won the second and last series of *Pop Idol*, a year later in 2003. The Glaswegian, dubbed by her neighbours as 'the wee lassie with the fantastic voice', had loved singing since she was a nipper and although happy with her life in Scotland, wanted to give the pop game a shot. As you do.

Like most hopefuls on these shows, Michelle had been trying to make it for years, trekking around Glasgow and Lanarkshire on the club circuit, supported by her parents and four younger sisters who made regular appearances in the crowd to cheer her on, to try to pave a way for herself in the music industry. After a while, she didn't think she was getting anywhere with her singing career.

Buoyed up by her friends who all believed she had what it takes to be a pop idol, Michelle watched Will take the *Pop Idol* crown and, with a few glasses of wine inside her, was encouraged to call up the number on the screen to get the audition form and apply for the second series to try to give her singing ambitions a boost.

"We were watching it and my friends were like, 'On you go!'," Michelle told *The Guardian*. "And I was like, 'No, I'd never get anywhere.' But because I had a wee bit of a drink in me, I phoned up and got an application form to fill out."

With that initial step made, Michelle auditioned in front of the judges in the Glasgow heat. Like Will Young before her, Michelle got a fair stick of headline-grabbing trouble during the auditioning process of *Pop Idol* and well up to the later stages of the competition. She even cited Will's career path and refreshing attitude as a positive influence over her during her early *Pop Idol* days. "I think Will is a great role model," she said. "There was all the talk about me not looking like a Pop Idol... and Will Young's not really taken that route either. He's really concentrated on the music and I think that's great."

Unlike Will, who was the first contestant to backchat Simon Cowell when the latter called his audition song 'distinctly average', simpering, "I don't think you could ever call that average," Michelle's future in the competition was left hanging in the balance. Judge Pete Waterman, as well as thinking her singing voice was nothing out of the ordinary – and nothing he couldn't hear belted out of any boozy karaoke competition down The Dog & Duck anywhere in the country – was concerned that she was too plump to be a pop success. "You're not a pop idol, you'll never be a pop idol," he said. And later, "You only had to look at her to know she was not a pop idol. Anyone who puts weight on during this competition ain't no pop idol."

Fellow judges Simon Cowell and Nicki Chapman were convinced that Michelle had the makings of a pop idol and championed her from the start, with his royal Simonness even later saying, "If you weren't in the final it would have been boring. You've broken the norm. I'm interested." The norm in that year's competition was contestants who were "freaks and geeks", according to Pete Waterman who moaned that "lots of kids that had a lot more musical integrity" had gone out of the competition well before their time in place of those "freaks and geeks".

Instead, the competitors included the 'ordinary bloke Idol' (©Simon Cowell, 2003) Mark Rhodes and, equally, his fellow contestant Sam Nixon who was also the vanilla, nice but standard sort of contestant you'd expect on this show. They were all eagerness and assertions that they'd dreamt of this moment since they were a little kid. (Indeed, a childhood dream that doesn't include wailing your heart out to a bored-looking Simon Cowell in front on a live studio audience surely isn't worth having these days.). They were enthusiastic enough about being on the show even when Simon likened Sam's performance to a 'bloke at a Christmas party' – mouldable and could hold a note.

The two singers, who met on the show and finished second and third respectively, have since gone on to have a longstanding career in children's TV, capitalising on their enthusiasm and playing the role of cheeky chappies. They come complete with kids' TV uniform of spiky hair, brightly coloured T-shirts and open-mouthed smiles and have become successful as presenters in that field. Move over the Chuckle Brothers.

They did give music a cursory shot after they were ejected from the competition but they packed it in pretty soon after releasing some bland covers of 'With A Little Help From My Friends' (which got to number one and included a video of the two friends grinning at each other, hardly believing their luck, and helping to impress yet further that this pair were pals and made a good duo if anyone out there had a job going for such a pair on a children's TV channel) and 'The Sun Has Come My Way' before finding their way into hosting kids' TV programmes like *Level Up* and *Sam And Mark's Guide To Dodging Disaster*. A testament to their success is that they were classified as stars and entered into the celebrity special of *Total Wipeout* in 2010 alongside Sally Gunnell, Danielle Lloyd and Joe Pasquale. Dizzy heights indeed.

Bucking the 'ordinary bloke idol' trend was the husky Susanne Manning, a singer whose raspy voice won over the judges, even reducing Pete Waterman to tears with her version of Rod Stewart's 'I Don't Want To Talk About It'. Susanne, who had previously split the judges between those who saw her as great potential – Simon, Nicki and Neil – and those who thought her music career was a "crazy dream" – Pete Waterman – then appeared to lose the support of the public after an alleged spat with Michelle McManus, which Susanne has denied ever since, and she was voted out of the competition despite being seen by many as a real contender for the title.

There was also Andy Scott Lee, brother of Steps singer Lisa and one-time member of 3SL (that's Three Scott Lees, compromised of him and his two brothers, Steve and Ant), who earns triple reality/talent TV points by also being Hear'Say singer Johnny Shentall as well as later being married, for 19 months, to Liberty X singer Michelle Heaton, and having an ITV documentary about their big day inexplicably called *Michelle And Andy's Big Day*. Andy's position in the competition was criticised because of his pop connections and previous recording contract.

There was also the 'vicar's son' Chris Hide whose sweet singing won him the respect of Pete Waterman who praised him "on behalf of the pensioners of Britain", but who was knocked out of the contest and finished in a very respectable fourth place. Kim Gee, a young mum-of-three from Grimsby – whose place in the pop competition was the cause of speculation because her figure was classified as larger than the average pop star's – looked like a strong contender in the contest but was booted out in the fifth week.

So it was then that hotel events manager Michelle, the bookies' rank outsider when she was put through to the top 12 finalists and who liked a glass of rosé on the weekend, enjoyed eating fry-ups and didn't take herself too seriously, became the fans' favourite with her sweetly sung Dina Carroll covers and effusive personality.

Indeed, rather than being the alleged underdog in the face of the standard pop of Sam and Mark, Michelle received the most votes six times out of a possible 11 live showdowns. Showing a graciousness about any negative comments – something she'd take with her and use for future jibes – plus a down-to-earth attitude that lent itself to the TV show and a drive to succeed having thus far found all doors shut for her, she was the clear winner in the show.

As well as capturing Simon Cowell's interest, Michelle was compared to Meatloaf and received a bouquet of flowers and message of support from the *Bat Out Of Hell* rocker when she won. She also had the then Scottish First Minister Jack McConnell praising her as a role model for young Scots as well as plaudits from Joan Bakewell, Tommy Sheridan, Esther Rantzen and health expert Professor Phil Hanlon, all admiring her for showing that people of all shapes and sizes can go on to achieve.

But no matter how well Michelle sang on the second series of *Pop Idol*, her singing was overshadowed by her appearance. Her outfits were ridiculed and her size was a constant reference point, even more so than Rik Waller who'd appeared in the first series of *Pop Idol* and also found his weight to be a subject of comment.

Rik eventually left *Pop Idol* after a severe bout of laryngitis, with former *Popstars* auditionee Darius Danesh taking his place. He has since gone on to capitalise on his size with appearances in ITV's *Celebrity Fit Club* where he was seen trying to squirm out of gruelling jogs around a field with Tory Ann Widdecombe on his tail – surely a good enough reason to bolt if there ever was one – and as a judge on a plus-size singing competition, *The XL Idol*, where contestants must be size 18 or over. As well as this, he scored a number six in the charts with Dolly Parton's much-covered 'I Will Always Love You' and jumped channels to go on Channel Five fly-on-the-wall programme *Back To Reality*, which featured stars of reality TV shows living together in a new reality TV show. Art imitating life imitating life. Or something.

Despite his weight often being a topic for discussion and using his size as a force for good in his career with *The XL Idol*, Rik was never made out to be a role model for young boys in the same way that Michelle was going against the grain of skinny minnie songstresses, nor was he ever told that his weight would stop him from being a singer.

Rik's weight was never held up as a challenge for stylists and nothing he wore was ridiculed; his default shiny blue shirt wasn't called a "tent" as it was for Michelle. "We [me and the stylist] have come up with some corkers that have been slagged in the press, but it's trial and error and now I've got much more say in what I'm wearing," she told *The Guardian*.

"There was a lot of focus on Rik Waller last year, but I think maybe not as much [as for a woman]," Michelle told *The Guardian*. "There's an image a girl's supposed to have. A lot of the women in pop look the same – they look fantastic, but they look the same – and if you don't fall into that category then you are going to stand out like a sore thumb.

"All the women Pete Waterman's dealt with were all similar – very small, very petite – and he's never dealt with someone like me before. But then Simon Cowell's done *American Idol* and some of the women in that were quite voluptuous, which opened his eyes.

"And Nicki Chapman is a woman so she understands that, as a woman, no matter what size or shape you are. everyone would love to change themselves and no one is really happy with how they look. That's a part of being a woman."

Refreshingly enough, Michelle always batted away any remarks about her figure as unimportant because she was happy with how she looked and didn't see it as much of a problem in the way that

Pete and others did. ("To be honest, I was quite happy being big so losing weight was never a consideration. I wasn't bullied at school and I enjoyed eating junk food," she told the NHS in an interview ahead of going on Channel 4 programme *You Are What You Eat)*.

Even better, she said that it would have been more upsetting and destructive for her if her singing talent was dismissed, and she refused to get bogged down with any negative feedback. "I'm very secure about how I look. I'd be much more upset if someone criticised my voice. You can always change your look – if you've got a crap voice that's it," she told *The Guardian* in 2003.

Even so, her weight would continue to be a huge feature in her career and is something she has struggled with in subsequent years. In the final show, where she was pitted against Walsall singer Mark Rhodes who was regularly in the bottom two or three of the votes, Pete still seemed surprised that Michelle had found her way to the final showdown.

When she won, there was much talk of it being a triumph for diversity and as proof that, as a nation, we wanted the most talented person to win and not just someone who looked like all the other prototype pop stars flooding the charts. We wanted our women to be the shape they were comfortable with and not one promoted by mass culture.

Even heart of gold Esther Rantzen patted the programme – and in particular judges Nicki Chapman and Simon Cowell who'd always backed Michelle – on the back for celebrating those who wouldn't usually have a chance to show off their talents on TV. Esther praised the programme's diversity as a breath of fresh air amid a predictable TV landscape. "*Pop Idol* blasts through the professional preconceptions, demolishes all the trite clichés regulating what an icon should look and sound like," she told the *Daily Mail*. "Pretentious pop pundits knock the show, accusing it of discovering bland, mediocre singers. It's been called 'an insipid, music industry conveyor belt'. In fact *Pop Idol's* crime is to break the mould and Michelle is the only evidence you need of that. She is a genuine talent and a refreshing change from so many synthesised hits."

When Michelle broke the mould and won the ITV final (a result that allegedly led judge Pete Waterman to stalk out of the studio) it might have made for a refreshing change but attention was once again shifted to her weight.

Michelle was even asked if she thought she'd picked up votes out of sympathy, presumably because Waterman, by no means a beginner in music and certainly well-respected and influential in the industry, was unsure whether she would make it in pop, and people had no doubt responded to this by voting in their millions in outrage. This is after five million people called up to pledge her as their favourite contestant. Five million is certainly a lot of people to make a sympathy call but yet again the focus was not on her upcoming music but her looks.

"I am part of the British public and we won't vote for people because we feel sorry for them, we vote for them because they are talented," she said after her win.

Talented though Michelle might have been, Aaron Bayley who was a finalist in the first series of *Pop Idol* and who went on to record music afterwards, reckons that she won the show because it made the programme look more representative of the nation, and showed that we were a fair and balanced bunch, even if in actuality we might have preferred one of the other finalists as the winner.

Aaron, who has been playing with a live band and writing songs, agrees with Pete Waterman that pop fans expect their pop stars to be slim and young, and that the industry – and the people who generally buy the albums the contestants produce – probably isn't that sympathetic towards those who fall outside of that, including both Michelle and first *X Factor* winner Steve Brookstein. Because of that, Aaron thinks the two winners were destined to have short careers in music because in the charts, the traditional pop star wins out.

"I strongly believe that the likes of Steve Brookstein and Michelle McManus were 'allowed' to win in order to prove a point," said Aaron. "The point was that the older generation and the slightly larger pop star were in with a chance of getting on these shows and winning them.

"However in the long term this was never going to be the case in the charts and they'll never win out in there because the general buying audience for these programmes are teenagers and in the cold light of day, they aren't going to buy the records of someone over the age of 20 or become a fan of anyone whose figure doesn't fit the ideal stereotype."

As bland as that idealised vision may be for pop, Aaron reckons that image can't be altogether dismissed. It is often an important factor in why some contestants and pop stars are popular in talent TV shows and retain the interest of the public despite not having as much musical flair as others. While diversity might look balanced on TV, in the pop charts Aaron thinks the standard pop star image will always win out because music fans buy into that image and regard it highly.

"In instances such as Michelle McManus and Steve Brookstein it isn't as much about talent as it is image," says Aaron. "Let's face it, Jedward from the sixth series of *The X Factor* are a prime example. Totally and utterly musically inept but for some reason they had an image that at the time was what some people liked and so they stayed in the competition."

While Michelle certainly wasn't musically inept, she was dogged with questions about her suitability as a pop idol when she won the show. Unusually, she was bombarded with question about her longevity as soon as she even released a single – and was probably the first talent TV contestant to have their career prospects cross-examined so thoroughly. Here, Pete Waterman, who'd kept quiet about Michelle's win for the first month after she won the show, also waded in, questioning her survival chances and suggesting that her career would be dust within a year of winning the show.

"The winner [of *Pop Idol* series two] was rubbish and I think her low sales probably reflect that," he said a month after Michelle's win. "She won't even last six months. He [Simon] wanted Michelle to win and she did. Will Young was a fantastic winner, Michelle is not.

Keep On ... *Pop Idol* winner Will Young has enjoyed a successful career in music and film.
(Ken McKay/Rex Features)

Idol ... Will Young awaits news of his fate on the first series of *Pop Idol*.
(*FremantleMedia Ltd/Rex Feature*)

Pop Ideal ... *Pop Idol* rivals Will Young and Gareth Gates maintained a friendship throughout the contest. (*Ken Towner/Evening Standard/Rex Features*)

Nerve wracking ... Contestants on the second series of *Pop Idol* are told who will go through to the next round. *(Ken McKay/Rex Features)*

Top Marks ... *Pop Idol* series two rivals Mark Rhodes, Michelle McManus and Sam Nixon pictured ahead of the series final. (*Ken McKay/Rex Features*)

Score ... Michelle McManus celebrates her *Pop Idol* win and subsequent success of her first single 'All This Time'. (*Darren Banks/Rex Features*)

Against All Odds ... *X Factor* winner Steve Brookstein celebrates his win with mentor Simon Cowell. (*Rex Features*)

Jack the lad ... *X Factor* winner Leon Jackson perfects his pop star smile.
(*Gregory Pace/BEI/Rex Features*)

Gee-d up ... *X Factor* runners-up G4 in concert. (*Huw John/Rex Features*)

That's My Goal ... *X Factor* winner Shayne Ward proudly holds his album *Breathless*.
*(Jeremy Craine/Rex Features)*

Brain Ward ... Shayne Ward in deep
concentration on stage.
*(Shirlaine Forrest/WireImage)*

O Fortuna ... *X Factor* runner up Rhydian
Roberts gets ready to perform. *(Rex Features)*

Superstar … *X Factor* winner Leona Lewis. [*Rex Features*]

Overcome … *X Factor* winner Alexandra Burke performs. *(Mark Allan/Wireimage)*

She is simply not a big talent and is certainly not a pop idol. Even the people of Scotland are bored with her."

Michelle's debut with the 'low sales' was 'All This Time', which both she and Mark Rhodes sang in the final of the show. Even if her former judge didn't think much of it, she was entered into the *Guinness Book Of World Records* for being the first Scottish female to get to number one in the UK charts with her debut single.

'All This Time' stayed at number one for three weeks and Michelle brought out her first album, *The Meaning Of Love*, six weeks after she took the 2003 *Pop Idol* title; it entered the charts at number three. She released another single, with the same name of the album, which got to number 16 in the charts. While having a Top 5 album and single and another top twenty single might sound like a massive achievement to most upcoming pop contenders, in the skewed world of TV talent shows it can be seen as a massive disappointment.

"The charts can be a hard place for new singers from these TV shows," says HMV's head of press Gennaro Castaldo. "Often, with someone like a *Pop Idol* winner they'll need to keep getting Top 5 hits to justify all the money that is spent on them, especially if they're not internationally successful like Leona Lewis or Alexandra Burke."

Other acts bringing out singles and albums around the time Michelle brought out hers might have whooped and cheered with joy at the chart success. Gennaro thinks that a succession of lower-ranking singles can spell disaster for a winner who will have had lots of money pumped into them to turn the songs into hits. "For other acts coming out recording similar music, they might be really pleased with getting to number 11," says Gennaro. "But the record label will have put more money and more feelers out about a winner's single than they might another contestant or a similar act and so understandably they will expect more return."

The lack of number ones can present a distinct problem when it comes to launching a winner's album. If their singles haven't done as well as expected – and with the demand for singles smaller than it's ever been – and if their album follows suit, then parting company might seem like the most reasonable option if all avenues had been explored.

"I think a problem a lot of contestants find is that nowadays the singles market is much smaller than it was say 20 years ago and often a lot of the money is made on tours and on albums," says Gennaro. "But for a pop singer from one of these shows to have a successful album they'll need to have three or four Top 5 or Top 10 singles and that can be difficult when by the time they've released their third single, the next year's winner is already out there and getting to number one and the attention on them drops off. So the interest in their album might dip and it might not do as well as expected. In a way, there's nothing that anyone can do about this unless your career takes off in a major way like that of Leona Lewis or Will Young. That's just the nature of these shows to bring new talent and new singers to the charts every year.

"It's different for bands because people buy their albums regardless of whether they have two or three good singles and they don't put so much importance on the chart entry of the single because they expect that the album will be good throughout and will stand alone. People don't do that as much with pop singers because they base their careers around bringing out great songs. With the singles market as it stands today, it can be hard to capture people's interest or have the impact they might have liked to have.

"These programmes do have arena tours but they are built around performing songs the contestants sang on the show with a few singles thrown in.

That's fine, people evidently like seeing the contestants doing that onstage and it makes sense to tour with that sort of show but it's easy to see that if a contestant hasn't already won people over with their debut album, that part of their career will be over soon because they haven't moved away from the TV show and done enough to warrant a career outside of it. They might not be able to sell as many tour dates of their own gigs off the back of their album."

Unfortunately for Michelle, she seemed to fit into this category of winner. A year after her win she was dropped by the label that signed her as part of her *Pop Idol* prize. To this day, Michelle thinks her label dropped her because of her size and how she looked rather than her musical credentials.

"My music wasn't successful because of the way I look, simple as that," she told *Closer* magazine. "I always knew I was going to struggle, and I never thought the press or public were wrong for slating me – it's all about image nowadays."

Michelle thinks that even Leona Lewis, possibly the greatest talent and success story to come out of a UK TV talent search, would have had trouble sustaining her career if she had been larger. "Leona Lewis' voice is miles better than mine – but Leona wouldn't be where she is now if she was 23 stone, like I was, when she won," she told *Closer.* "The record companies wouldn't have stood by her. Mine didn't. It's hard to market a larger female singer – it's not as if I could do a calendar in my smalls!"

With no calendars to her name and an ailing album, Michelle found alternative management and worked with them on her second album, which is scheduled for release in 2010. She even found an ally in Sir Elton John who said he hated the way in which contestants were treated and how soon their careers went into decline, especially when they had talent like Michelle.

"The record companies sell a lot of records and those people are gone. It's f★★★ing cruel," Elton told *The Mirror.* "Look at Michelle McManus. My heart bleeds for her. She won *Pop Idol,* she's a really good singer and now she's forgotten."

Michelle shrugged off the suggestions that she'd been mistreated by the programme and said she'd found *Pop Idol* a positive experience and was determined to make it in the industry and not be forgotten. She said she would do this with confidence and determination to succeed.

Regardless of her confidence and determination, and putting aside the lack of posing in lingerie for calendar shoots, Fraser McAlpine thinks that Michelle was given the wrong type of songs to sing and was marketed in a way that was out of touch with the charts at that point. As such, pop fans would have lost interest in her music early on because there were plenty of other singers doing something more interesting and contemporary. They might not have had the patience to wait around while the lady from *Pop Idol* got her records in order.

"*Pop Idol* and the record label didn't seem to have a clue what to do with Michelle McManus," says Fraser. "At that point, she was the first female winner of the show and of the show's genre. Yet they used the same model that they used for male singers, which was to market her as a one-woman Westlife. You know, a few ballads with the predictable key change, soppy lyrics and the standard talent show video of that time; sitting on stool or in a darkened room with pictures of her on the show flashing up in the background."

While Michelle's singing style worked on television, and a few cleverly placed key changes and lyrics that related to the lessons learned on the show are effective enough on the box, in the charts it fell apart because the pop market had moved on to something else and her career stumbled because she couldn't recapture that. "The problem is that the music Michelle was releasing was really unfashionable by then," says Fraser. "That wasn't her fault but I just don't think they knew how to market her or what to do with winners at that point because the genre was in its infancy and they weren't sure what would sell with winners.

"So Michelle was treated in the same way that male singers were treated but that Westlife format was old five years before Michelle came out of *Pop Idol*. It didn't work because it didn't suit her and it didn't work with her personality or with what was popular then."

While Michelle points to her figure as the principal factor in her music career ending sooner than she might have wanted, Fraser thinks that her distinctive look and the fact that people were talking about her might have been a blessing in disguise, even if some of the comments were negative.

"Michelle's size had little to do with her music career being over quickly," says Fraser. "In fact, in a way it might have been beneficial to her because she stood out and because people remembered her, which is more than most people do with contestants and winners because there have been so many of them."

Ultimately though, Fraser thinks that being likeable and going on a TV show can only get you so far before fans move on, simply because there are plenty of other likeable people who go on TV shows and make music. And with the Noughties being the decade of people making a name for themselves without the backing of a record label or a giant TV brand, pop fans would naturally expect more of the singer who'd had all that label support than an act who'd done it all their own way.

"Michelle McManus never really moaned about the show that made her name," says Fraser. "This has probably kept her in well-regard with a lot of people, particularly those who voted for her. These shows are massively popular and if you come out of a programme slagging it off you're going to ruffle a lot of people's feathers.

"Surprisingly enough, she never really rose to any of the comments about her looks, which must have been hurtful. But while she may have come across well on TV and may have stayed down-to-earth and upbeat, the songs weren't good enough and that's what pop fans latch on to.

"They can only care so much about someone being a nice person or someone winning a TV show. But if after three or four songs they're still not making the type of music that matters to fans, then they'll move on to someone else who does sing songs that they deem to be good. Besides which, we don't always want nice pop stars who we can relate to; we want them to have bizarre hobbies, say outlandish things and be different from us. That's what makes them fun and interesting."

Family band Voices With Soul, consisting of Grace, Hildia and Corene Campbell, appeared on the first series of *The X Factor* and are still busy now playing at soul nights, private parties in Cannes and Barbados and are putting together an album. They believe that the hardest work for contestants comes after the show has finished. Without the best songs and direction, Michelle's career stalled at the time it needed to be pushed.

"We always say that the hard work comes after you leave the show," says Corene Campbell. "When you're in the programme, you might be stressed out because you know you're performing to millions of people but you still have all the backing of the judges and viewers and you get the chance to perform and show what you can do.

"It's when you come out and you've got to make it on your own and keep getting out there that's the problem. People think you've died or stopped recording music all together if they don't hear about you in the papers all the time. They'll stop us and say, 'Oh you're still together as a band, I didn't realise', and we get a good reaction from them when they know we're still going but they expect that you've fallen off the face of the earth if you haven't got your face splashed over the magazines."

So Michelle, who seemingly stopped appearing on the box every week and who changed management, may have found that she needed to toil away harder than ever before to make people aware that she was still around.

"We've been really busy since leaving the programme," says Corene. "We still sing together, record together and do a lot of corporate parties but the hard work is letting people know that you're still around and still singing even if you're not on the telly every week. That has to come from you. It's no good expecting that all this will happen because you've been on TV and you can't expect that Simon Cowell and everyone else on the show will sign you and take you under their wing because there are so many acts and contestants that it would be impossible for them to do that for everybody. You have to see the show as a great starting point to your career.

"It doesn't mean that you'll get everything handed to you on a plate and that you'll get the big recording deal and tours. But you have to plug away at it and keep at it because if you don't, it could be all over. People still remember us from *The X Factor* and we were on the very first series and didn't win or come runners up. We've kept busy, we had a good profile on the programme and kept at it and I think that helps."

Too many other *Pop Idol, Fame Academy* and *X Factor* contestants infiltrating the pop market meant that Michelle was pushed out of the way, and her apparent drift from music to TV presenting meant she was no longer associated with actually singing. With the internet changing the face of pop and her more modest music career with her new label, she was no longer this year's hot property. "As it is the nature of these shows, that next person who grabs the interest of pop fans is usually a contestant or a winner from the next year's talent search," says Fraser McAlpine. "By that point, if you haven't released good enough songs or brought anything new out, then you're pretty much forgotten about.

"People have a different series or winner in mind when they think of the programme. That aspect of your career is over because all these other people have the same TV foundations as you had so you can't really rely on your TV background any more, which is what you might have been doing up until that point. It's a shame for them.

"But then, if you look at where pop is at the moment, you've got singles sales down, album sales down and people springing up putting their songs on the internet and getting noticed that way by fans all over the world. It is the fans they are responding with and who are making them relevant. In comparison, releasing a couple of covers of ballads off the back of a TV programme you went on looks really stale."

James Fox, a contestant on the second series of *Fame Academy*, has since gone on to have success with his two albums, tours, a Eurovision Song Contest entry and a stint in the West End. He thinks that the reason Michelle didn't go on to a longer career in music was because she didn't seem to have a very clear idea of the type of songs she wanted to perform afterwards, unlike Will Young before her who always seemed to have a very sharp sense of what sort of artist he wanted to be.

Without songs or the skills to write great pop songs or even knowing what songs A&R men prefer, it can be hard for a singer to get back into the industry, or at least get back to the top of the charts. Once that happens, it can be difficult for winners to get past the fact that their career is more low-key than it once was. Fans will think they've failed if they don't have the all-singing all-dancing career with bells on top, and that oft used 'double edged sword' situation comes into its own here.

"Michelle McManus was a great singer but what she had in common with Alex Parks from *Fame Academy* was that she wasn't too sure of the direction she wanted to take her music in," says James. "You know, if you left Michelle and Alex in a room on their own for the next 10 years, would they come up with an album? Probably not.

"Maybe I'm being too harsh here because I do think they're both great singers but great singers need great songwriters to move their careers along. Having a nice voice and winning a TV programme isn't enough for record buyers and it isn't enough for labels if they've tried it with you and it hasn't worked out."

James thinks the reason for Michelle's exit from music at the time of writing is down to a lack of opportunities to work with the kind of songwriters and producers that may be afforded to the winner after first scooping the prize but will soon diminish if they don't continue to sell. As soon as the next winner comes along the focus turns to getting their careers on the right tracks.

"People aren't rushing out to write songs for Michelle McManus because there have been plenty of other winners since her and people are more interested in them," says James. "Those winners might have more idea of the songs they want to record and they're the next big thing so understandably the songwriters, musicians and producers want to work with them instead.

"The market for winners from these shows is over-saturated so whether you sink or swim is in the lap of the gods I guess. It's a tough one because Michelle does have a great voice but that's how it goes sometimes. It's been years since she won *Pop Idol* and there have been so many winners and contestants since then that what she's done has become a little lost in it all."

But even after Michelle's singing career took a hiatus Pete Waterman stuck to his guns in an interview with the *Daily Record,* insisting that although she was a 'sweet girl' she had turned attention away from singing on *Pop Idol* and as a result the programme had become more of a TV drama than it was supposed to be. "I lost interest in these shows when Michelle McManus won it because to me that was about TV – it wasn't about music," he told the paper.

Having, according to Pete Waterman, changed the emphasis on TV talent searches, Michelle stopped her music career in its tracks and concentrated on a career in TV presenting back in her native Scotland, while her runners up, Sam and Mark, continued to host children's TV shows. The contestants who are still plugging away at the music in the second series of *Pop Idol* finished much further down in the ranks.

That's not to say that contestants can't change their minds within the space of winning the show and being out in the big, bad world or, indeed, go back to music in the future, but it seems that they often make more of a career in areas other than singing: appearing on reality TV shows where they're challenged to eat slugs, fitness videos, West End shows and advertising brands of tights or soft drinks, all of which move them away from what was once their 'undying love', ie music.

Gossip writer Mr Holy Moly thinks that this career about-turn is inevitable given that the contestants have now wised up to the career options that follow a TV talent show. It might mean putting singing on the back burner and fronting a game show for a while but doing that means that at least they don't have to go crawling back to their old boss, tail between their legs, asking for their old job back.

"All the contestants are wise to these programmes," says Mr Holy Moly. "They know it's a TV show and they know they won't have that long outside of the show to make a career for themselves. Lucie Jones from the sixth series of *The X Factor* was a good singer who got booted out pretty early on. She's now got a modelling contract and is pretty happy because at least she doesn't have to go back on the dole. So the contestants do it for what they can get. Fame is like a drug; they have a taste of it and they want more. They play the NEC or whatever and they want more of it and so they do whatever they can to sustain it."

The singing career that Michelle so desperately wanted at the start of the decade might have diminished now but at least, as Mr Holy Moly says, she has sustained her profile and hasn't had to sign on.

# Chapter 6

# *The X Factor* Series One

When the dying embers of Hear'Say's pop career went shimmering up the chimney, their abrupt end ought to have spelled out a warning for the more cautious wannabes, but for others the chance to have their flights of fancy turned into reality was too good an opportunity to miss and well, they were different to Hear'Say, weren't they? It was a different programme for one. A whole different kettle of reality TV fish. This was more about the talent than the reality element.

Perhaps they were buoyed up by the success of Will Young – and his bold assertion to the BBC that, "Hear'Say were chosen by judges", and that success of an act cultivated on the telly might have more longevity if they were chosen by the people who watched the show and who might reasonably be expected to buy their tunes afterwards and not just by a gaggle of pop stars and industry insiders. Pah, what do they know anyway?

The triumphs of Gareth Gates, the cat o'nine ITV programme lives Darius Danesh from *Pop Idol* and the consistently brilliant Girls Aloud from *Popstars: The Rivals* might have given the thousands who turned up at regional auditions for their shot of glory on *The X Factor* a hit of confidence to burst right through those doors. Any niggling doubts in the form of One True Voice, Michelle McManus and Hear'Say, the whopping great elephants in the room of the genre, could be shrugged off in time for a quick blast of Whitney Houston and a public pleading with the judges.

Besides, the contenders could surely rely on the great British public to back them through the competition and in the outside world. After all, didn't those wise folk who spun proverbs also say haste is waste and time waits for no man, so get on *The X Factor* while you can?

One of those to have a pop at *The X Factor* was Steve Brookstein. A mid-thirties singer from South London, Steve had been skirting around the edges of musical success for years, performing and working with producers and writers. After being dropped by a label in the mid-Nineties he decided to turn producer, but found the music business increasingly hard as the years crept by and nippers were snapped up and signed in preference to the more mature performers.

So when *The X Factor* came along, he gave it a go and auditioned like thousands before him, all willing the famous faces on the panel to like them enough to keep them in the show. Only, Steve's first audition didn't go to plan. A seemingly louche entrance and ho-hum attitude led then judge Sharon Osbourne and fellow panellist Louis Walsh to proclaim that he lacked drive, had a "defeatist attitude" and didn't care enough about being a superstar to warrant further auditioning for their show. They shook their heads and sent him on his way. *The X Factor* needed people with drive and ambition not half-hearted chancers. And, FYI, there were plenty of people outside their doors who did have the drive.

But one judge believed that underneath this laid-back entrance, Steve Brookstein did have the ambition to take him from a pub singer vying for a bit of acclaim to a superstar. Simon Cowell called Steve back into the room and insisted on him coming back the following day to have another crack at impressing Louis and Sharon, who along with Simon were still chewing the fat about him long after he'd left the room for a natter with then-presenter Kate Thornton.

Steve came back and, luckily for him, impressed Louis and Sharon sufficiently for them to give him their blessing to go through to the next round. So it was that Steve came to be on the box every week, singing his heart out, treading a steady path to success as the cheeky chappie, a sure-fire way to win over voters and fans. Steve was congenial and seemed a deserving finalist, if not as compelling as ex-Happy Mondays singer Rowetta Satchell or the captivating rock-star-in-waiting Tabby Callaghan, who were an altogether different breed of artist not seen on talent TV before.

Steve's solid performances of soul classics proved he could sing well (phew) and could perform to a crowd, both of which are presumably key attributes in becoming a pop star. But other than that, it would be the final and his career afterwards that most viewers will remember about him.

Asked about her opinions after his final performance, Sharon gave Steve a dressing down, informing one and all that he was full of "BS" (bullshit), "fake" and "average". Many observers commentating on the outcome of the show cited her tongue-lashing as the reason voters rallied behind him. Sharon, never one to admit defeat, would later point out in her autobiography that Steve had the highest number of votes out of all the contestants to stay in week after week and her rebuke did nothing to encourage floating voters to get behind him, they were behind him anyway.

On the big night, six million cast votes to make him the winner, which still stands as the highest number of votes cast in a final of the show. It seems unlikely that six million people would vote purely out of pity.

After the incident, Sharon told *The Daily Mail* that she'd since mulled over the finale and decided she had got too personally involved in the show and let things get to her. In any case, she still believes that Steve Brookstein won the show fair and square because people wanted him to win and they thought he deserved it, and not because they were looking to give twos up to her feelings about him. "Ozzy told me I got far too emotionally involved with the show. He's right," Sharon told the *Mail*. "It should have been pure business, and it wasn't because I let it get personal."

Although this isn't an exact science, it is conceivable that some votes may have been cast in Steve's favour after Sharon's outburst. In some respects it is refreshing to hear such openness, even if it does appear a little uncomfortable amid the blandness created by intense media training, and Sharon's fizzling personality certainly makes for exciting TV. However, many commentators drew the conclusion that fans and viewers at home rallied around Steve, the perceived underdog, not because we thought he had the *X Factor* – though we might have thought he was a jolly good egg – but because we want to see our underdogs flourish and triumph in the face of adversity.

The UK loves an underdog. Give us someone on telly with two left feet or four left feet in the case of Jedward, series six finalists on *The X Factor,* some unusual yet endearing hand signals à la Same Difference from series four and some bonkers self-penned pop songs about it being cuckoo o'clock, or Chico Time as it came to be known when series two contestant Chico released it as a single, and we're all over them. "Oh yeah," we'll say to those we work with on a Monday morning. "Did you see so and so on *The X Factor* Saturday? I hated them last week. They were right annoying little gits but their version of Geri Halliwell's 'Scream If You Want To Go Faster' where they irritated the bejesus out of Simon Cowell and scooted around the stage on roller-skates was the bomb."

Likewise, an underdog on the box is a powerful beacon to viewers who vote with their emotions, even if it is just casting a vote so they can stay in another round of the show. And for a short while, it seemed like Steve Brookstein, the nice but steady underdog in the final compared with his enthralling peers, might just go on to dominate the charts and become the massive success the voters expected him to become, and so the rightful order of pop would be established across the land and we could all go home happy.

He was our sort of underdog and, after all, this was *The X Factor,* the show that would find a hitherto undiscovered talent with that, well, zig-a-zig-ah X factor thingumabob that no one really knows how to pinpoint until they see it coming smack, bam in the face – aha, that's your x factor for you – and when it does it should make us all proud to be living in a country where a castle in the sky becomes hard reality and a soundtrack to hum along to on the M25 in the process.

Besides, Brian from Westlife had hotfooted it off with Kerry Katona and left the band and their chart-friendly hits for good. Pop in 2004 was shaky and needed a new hero armed with some rousing soul-affirming tunes. And DJ Casper of the 'Cha Cha Slide' fame it wasn't.

So it seemed only right when Steve Brookstein's debut single went to number one a week after its Christmas release in 2004, though he was initially pipped to the top spot by the rag-tag string of pop stars singing on the reincarnation of 'Do They Know It's Christmas?' 20 years after the original supergroup first brought out that charity single.

Following the tradition of talent TV winners releasing songs heavily laden with metaphors of toiling hard and coming up against nay-sayers, Steve's first single was a cover of Phil Collins' 'Against All Odds (Take A Look At Me Now)'. Sung by Steve, or indeed any talent TV show winner, it came to represent the show's core values.

A video was made that spliced black and white footage of Steve being turned down by Louis Walsh with scenes of him being told he'd made it through to the next round – against all odds – to, finally, colour footage of him winning the show, looking all moody in a suit – a rite of passage for any self-respecting male singer hoping to flog a few albums, jeans just aren't swoonsome enough – and clips of him performing his song to a rapturous TV crowd who had made him the winner. Against. All. Odds.

In fairness to those behind the choice of songs and direction of the video, they are effective and presumably easy to bash out in time for the Christmas singles rush. Otherwise why would they produce them year after year? Besides, after all the pomp of the show, it'd be foolish to bring out a lavish video and song that didn't capitalise on the idea of dreams slipping through fingers. With the world and its mother telling them to stop idling the day away dreaming of being a pop star, being able to find the strength to grab it back and come back mightier than ever makes a compelling script. But, crucially, it must show that he hadn't lost his 'common touch' when 'walking with kings' or, in this case, Kate Thornton and Simon Cowell, and that beneath it all, they were the very same person who auditioned months ago. Because no one likes a big head or a smart alec winner. *The Apprentice*, this is not.

The videos play on the dream of someone brought off the street with wild fantasies of singing professionally packed up in a very stirring collection of sound bites that reaffirm to us at home that we have made the right decision in voting for them. They cut to the contestant in that big bad world of reality telly where people can give them a dressing down every week and rain on their parade but then, eventually, they belt out a ballad that stops them in their tracks and makes everyone at home say, yes, yes he has that previously inexplicable *X Factor* malarky they were banging on about. I. Get. It. Now. Well done Steve Brookstein and well done us for spotting his talent.

This is Steve Brookstein's video all over. It's a sort of handy digest of Steve's four months on *The X Factor*, useful for those not glued to the telly or whose video recorder or digital box didn't work who might be wondering, "Who the heck is this Steve Brookstein chap?"

The heartstring-pulling cover single was released, complete with its very apt video and Steve scored his first number one, which, for what anyone might say about his career after *The X Factor* and about the charts being meaningless, is still no shabby achievement. Later on, in May of that year, Steve's first album, *Heart And Soul*, was released. It went to number one.

But all that glitters isn't gold. Or indeed isn't platinum or double platinum. Steve's debut album with Sony may have gone to number one when it was released and achieved gold status, but he still wasn't happy with things. Runners-up G4, an opera-singing quartet, all suits, please and thank yous and winning smiles, brought out their eponymous album to coincide with Mother's Day in March, ensuring a massive boost of sales. It went double platinum. Steve's went gold.

From the off, Steve believes the May release of his album didn't help win him fans or give him the level of success expected of a winner. He says he was portrayed as a cheeky chappie, the sort of loveable rogue that many ladies of a certain age would gush over and coo happily if they'd been given his album for Mother's Day. But rather than reap that cash cow in the run-up to Mother's Day, his album came out two months later, and by then all the mums were humming along to G4's version of 'Nessun Dorma'.

"I was always branded the housewives' favourite – cheeky smile, romantic songs – so you would've thought that my album would come out on Mother's Day, the biggest selling point of the year," Steve told *The Guardian*. "G4 released their album for Mother's Day and sold a quarter of a million records in a week. My album came out for Father's Day. Why? Thanks, guys. Are you trying to screw me over? I said: 'You're trying to ruin my career.' And I'm branded as bitter. Well, no shit, Sherlock! It did take a long time to be philosophical, and not be angry about it."

Anger turned to disputes at the record label as Steve fought to include more original songs on the second album as well as a few classic covers with his own spin on them, while Sony stuck to its guns and reportedly insisted that the second album would be more covers of well-loved songs so they could pander to the market they'd already captured on the show.

A second single never materialized, meaning his first single release was his last with the label. No sooner was the comforting carpet of stardom and music fame placed beneath Steve's feet than it was whipped away and he was left back at square one. Eight months after winning the show, Steve shipped out of Sony BMG.

"I wanted to go one way," he told *News Of The World* at the time, "and he [Simon] wanted me to go another. So we parted."

Simon Cowell later told the *Daily Mail* that Steve had begrudged the show and was blaming his misgivings on it rather than because the public had never taken him to their hearts as much as he expected. "Steve Brookstein, the winner of the first ever *The X Factor,* has been going around saying that whole show is just a cynical money-making exercise," Cowell told the paper. "Steve is not a happy bunny. He never was. He is just a bitter man who the public never warmed to. Steve proved to me that just because you have a winner, it does not always mean that you have a star."

Blimey. Daniel Evans was a contestant on the fifth series of *The X Factor* and has since been playing gigs and recording his first album. On Steve, David thinks that it's hard for winners to have a say in their career and as soon as they do, it can turn against them. "The winners have no say in their musical direction," says Daniel. "The last time someone tried to have a say, he was dropped within three months, remember Steve Brookstein?"

Daniel on the other hand, as a non-winner, is content having greater scope for doing whatever he darned well feels like. Sure, the fanfare that the winners trail might not be there, but then the expectations and limitations aren't there either. It has worked for him anyway.

"I did my album and every note, the printing, the arrangements, the musicians were all my choice," says Daniel. "Despite the fact it will never be mainstream – that's impossible without a label backing you as they also control a lot of what is heard on the radio – it is something I am proud of and can play to my kids when I'm old and say, 'That was all my own choices and my work.' Not many people can say that of their albums."

Who knows? Maybe Steve Brookstein has had enough distance to feel proud of his first long-player. Regardless of this, Fraser McAlpine, thinks that Steve's decision to go it alone rather than play along with the career he'd been given – and the pasting he got for doing so – makes him talent TV's biggest casualty. He may be content with the music he is making now but his lack of chart success seems to be viewed as evidence that he is no longer alive in the pop world.

"Steve Brookstein was the underdog in *The X Factor* because he was that bit older. He seemed to know what was going on and, in that sense, he is the person I most feel for in this," says Fraser. "He didn't seem as excited to be there as some of the other contestants, maybe because he had already been in the business for a while and was disillusioned with it.

"But when he came out, he wasn't the underdog any more. He'd won the show and was due to reap the rewards and all the success that was supposed to go with it, but instead he was still being thrashed in the charts by G4. He wanted to do his own thing. He wasn't happy with the songs he was given and he reacted to that and left.

"His label, Sony, had its views on the music he should record but it's always going to be that bit more difficult to reach an agreement between a label and a singer when the singer is that bit older and knows himself a bit better and has been around the block in the music industry before.

"Steve Brookstein wasn't as mouldable as some of these people who apply, the Leon Jacksons and Joe McElderrys of this world; young, probably just finished their A-levels or college and have no prior music experience. Steve Brookstein wasn't that type of contestant. Both parties thought they were right and weren't going to back down."

While Simon Cowell and his fellow judges are media darlings so highly prized that they can do several interviews a week where they can amend their quotes, Steve Brookstein had no realistic opportunity to do that should he have wanted to. The only way he could let his feelings be known was by telling all and sundry about his experience, but when he did that it sounded like he was whinging and, since most people know him solely for *The X Factor*, being ungrateful.

"The only way Steve can retaliate now is by bringing out that music he wanted to do in the first place, but at the same time he'll need the publicity to get that music out there," says Fraser. "Inevitably, when he does talk, he'll mention *The X Factor* or they'll mention *The X Factor* because that's how he came to the public's notice and when this happens and he talks about it, it has a propensity to sound like carping and who wants to listen to carping?

"More importantly it looks ungrateful. People aren't going to want to support his career if he sounds ungracious about what he's been given as a result of going on a hugely popular TV show. Those who voted for him had a sort of stake in him when he was in the show. It's not like there's a shortage of people who have the same ambition as he did, which is to make a living out of singing, and they had no obligation to keep spending money on voting him in.

"I can really appreciate why Steve Brookstein would be annoyed by the way things turned out and he has every right to feel that way, but on the other hand the people who have spent money calling in, voting for him above other people and who were interested in his career at the very beginning, might get narked with him because they might feel like he didn't appreciate them voting for him. They might also feel that, well he's had a number one single, it didn't work out afterwards, but he had a shot at making it in the music industry. How many people get a shot like that? Not many.

"If he could come back, make music he believed in and was recognised for that, that would be brilliant. But I don't think that's going to happen and if he does, he'll still be associated with the show that he appears to now dislike.

"Either way, Simon Cowell wins. Simon will still look like the good guy in it all because he helped Steve achieve some success off the back of the show and Steve didn't want to follow what he had laid out for him. You can argue the merits of that but because of the show, and in a way because of Simon Cowell, he had a number one single and a number one album.

"Simon doesn't have to react to what Steve's doing now because in a way, Steve rejected all that, and consequently rejected that success. And because he can get away with not mentioning Steve, he can talk about all the successes he has had and not sound bitter about him.

"But should we judge Steve Brookstein harshly for deciding he didn't want to play that particular game? No. It would have been easier for him to agree and just sit back, put a nice suit on, croon the covers, smile sweetly at grannies and get on with that Westlife model of doing things. But he didn't so I think we should respect him."

Whether a new artist who hadn't been through a TV show and

who didn't want to comply with his manager's orders would have been thus mocked for having done an about-turn is anyone's guess. But would Steve's peers have done the same if they'd been offered a second album with Sony BMG?

Tabby Callaghan, who came third in *The X Factor* in Steve's year, believes the winner made the wrong decision. Tabby thinks that with a show like *The X Factor*, if you've won and are an artist like Steve, the key thing is just to play along with the game until you have a chance and do your own thing later down the line when you have the resources to do so and have met the right people to help you make the music you want to make

"Personally, I think Steve Brookstein was wrong in not bringing out a second album of covers," says Tabby. "If you win *The X Factor* and Simon Cowell wants to work with you, you know what to expect but you take the work while it's there because if you are the type of artist that Steve is, you don't know how long the work will be there so you do it.

"Yeah, they will get you to release an album of cheesy covers or something like that, something popular and likely to sell. Simon'll get you to sing in a nice suit and have you looking clean cut. But he'll get you talking about your single and performing it on all the TV shows and then the single's out there and hopefully you'll have a success on your hands.

"You don't know what's around the corner in this business. It's fickle. It changes often and tastes change, so you do that type of album if you are that type of artist because it gives you the success that was talked about on the show. It opens doors for you later on and if you've won, presumably you'll want to stay in the spotlight for a little longer and you'd probably expect to be popular for longer, so you do it.

"That's fine though. I'm not that type of artist but there is a place for that type of album and there's a place for that type of artist just as there's a place for artists and albums completely different to that. If you win *The X Factor* then chances are you will be doing an album similar to that and chances are you will be that sort of artist.

"I just think if Simon Cowell is giving you the chance to work with him, then you grab it with both hands because he'll put you in touch with producers and songwriters and you'll get your songs out there. You'll get to be a singer and a singer who can make a living out of his career.

"Simon's a smart businessman and when he's looking at acts he's looking at the business potential so even if the act he and his company are promoting isn't massively talented or even original, they'll give them a song that will maximise their potential to get number ones in the charts and that is usually by giving them a cover or a ballad.

"There's a saying for someone like Simon Cowell: he could fall in shit and come up still smelling of roses. It's true. He's the winner out of it all. He makes the money and is successful but then he is honest about the fact that he wants to make shitloads of money and be successful and that he wants the winner to have successful albums even if that means making music you don't necessarily like.

"If someone comes on *The X Factor* or a similar show and they haven't grasped that and that it's about making money, then they're on the wrong programme."

Quite. Series five contestant Austin Drage reckons that while he can understand Steve Brookstein's desire to put his own thumbprints on his career, it was no surprise that after playing ball with the first album his record label didn't want to give him the reins. After all, they have experience and knowledge of what works and if something's not broken why fix it?

"I've read a lot in the papers about Steve Brookstein being dropped because he didn't like the music the label had been giving him," says Austin. "Sometimes if you've made it in a certain way, being a certain type of artist, it's usually the way people – fans, the label, media – expect you to carry on going.

"The label isn't going to want to suddenly let you start writing your own songs and going in your own direction if it's different from the one that was originally set for you... ultimately, it's a business for them and if they let everyone go off and do their own thing, they probably wouldn't get much money back. But they know that they're making a lot of money while you sing the songs that work. If people didn't like it, they wouldn't buy it.

"As for the record label, as long as they're making money out of that type of artist, then they're happy. So unless from the start you have had control over your style and song choice, then it will be hard to claw back some later on."

Without hindsight or this guidance, Steve went his own way and remains resolute that his decision was the right one. In fact, *The X Factor* seems to have helped sharpen his ambition and realise exactly what it is that he does and doesn't want to do in life; a steep learning curve maybe but one all the same.

"Simon Cowell put me into suits," Steve told *The Guardian* in 2008. "He said, 'We want you to look and dress and act like a star.' I took that on board. When he asked me to do stuff that wasn't befitting of a star, I thought, no, you wouldn't have Michael McDonald, or any of my heroes, going to Mavis on checkout five and singing."

Indeed, and so Steve left the supermarket checkouts to harried customers and ex-soap stars looking to launch new products in return for a pretty penny and some nice local publicity, and parted company with Simon and Sony BMG. Taking a back-to-basics approach, Steve threw himself into gigging and making music on his own terms, with none of the schmaltz he appeared to dislike from his Sony days.

But turning your back on a massive record deal and music love-in with Simon Cowell is never going to look like the wisest of moves to all the fans you've gathered off the back of Simon Cowell's show.

Reasonably enough, they may feel miffed because they quite liked you as a complicit *X Factor* winner who sang rather nice soul covers and who fell into line, played nicely and marched to the same beat as winners of similar shows. And if that means wearing a nice suit – what's wrong with a nice suit? – and visiting supermarkets to sing to Mavis on aisle five and crooning covers, then so be it.

Still, that beat wasn't right for Steve but he still had fans who were interested in his new direction and so he laid on a tour. Unfortunately for Steve, his first tour since leaving the label suffered from low attendances at some venues. He believed that this was down to poor promotion and a lack of proper ticket-selling procedures and not because he'd lost the majority of his well-wishers.

"I don't know what's going on," said Steve at the time of his sparsely attended gig in Worthing. "But the tour is being really badly promoted. I am really disappointed. People, even my friends, aren't able to buy tickets, even when they are available. It's promotional incompetence and I'm getting shafted left, right and centre. Other gigs are doing much better, though, and the actual show is amazing, which, as far as I'm concerned, is what it's all about."

Steve released *40,000 Things*, his first album after his split with Sony, independently but it only reached number 165 in the charts, selling 1,000 copies compared with *Heart And Soul*'s towering 250,000. Then he talked about how disillusioned he was with the show and its aftermath, but by that point it was time for the next series of *The X Factor* and most fans had turned their attentions toward the new throng of warbling wannabes. He wanted to do his thing, fine, but it wasn't going to stop the rest of the UK from enjoying the second series.

"For two years after the show, all the negativity that came my way made me very depressed," Steve told the *Daily Record*. "I don't do drugs, so I ate a lot and put on two and a half stone. It was depressing, but through it all you keep going thanks to the strength of family and, luckily, I'm feeling a lot better now. I went into *The X Factor* with confidence but after I won it, I lost a lot of it."

Fortunately, Steve rebuilt his confidence and a role in the musical *Our House* helped boost his ego. He'd had a rough time but he had got over the worst of it. But should we really judge Steve so harshly? At a time in his career when he could quite easily have said yes to the suits, the covers, the cosying up to presenters on late-afternoon chat shows, he stood up for himself and said he didn't want to make music that he didn't believe in and be the type of artist he wasn't. It might have cost him his contract at Sony BMG and invites to premieres, but he moved into an area that suited him better.

There are scores of bands who, once they've had a number one album and have their songs blaring out on popular TV shows, then bang on about the importance of 'staying true' to themselves and berate 'manufactured pop' and TV shows like *Pop Idol* or *The X Factor*. Then they give those songs that bleat about not 'selling out' and sticking it to 'the man' to mobile phone companies keen to use a song such as that to give the impression of being down with the kids.

Or bold as brass, go on *The X Factor* and sing that song, eager to get a slice of the pie. How many of those bands and singers could truly say that if they were offered a hero's wage and international fame they would have turned it down?

Likewise, the same papers, radio stations and TV shows who praised Steve when he won the show, hung out the bunting and made him their darling, now point and laugh at him for playing to smaller crowds in pizza restaurants. "I sing at restaurants and birthday parties, which keeps me ticking over, but I'm scared the minute I do a gig *The Mirror* will be there to take the piss, 'Steve Brookstein working the pubs again,'" Steve told *The Times*.

But if Steve, who now runs his own record label, is singing music he feels proud of, earns his keep and the people who now support him do so because they like his music and not just because he was on the telly once, then shouldn't we be applauding him rather than knocking him down?

Austin Drage, who is now recording and making music with a band, reckons that we should cut Steve some more slack because, after all, he's doing what he always wanted to do: sing.

"Steve Brookstein is still gigging," says Austin. "I hear about him doing sets in piano bars and having a great time and I think good luck to him. I think he obviously still likes playing and performing so why shouldn't he carry on gigging just because the places he now plays aren't Wembley? Big deal.

"He obviously loves what he does so much that he does the behind the scenes stuff like producing his wife Jackie's album. He doesn't need to have people screaming at him all day long that they love him. This is his life now.

"Don't get me wrong it's nice to have people support you but it shouldn't be about that. It should be about loving what you do and doing it because of that and not because you get invited to parties or because you get your pictures in the paper. People support you because they can see you love what you do and it shines through and hopefully the people who follow Steve Brookstein can see that he loves what he does and support him because of that. Fair play to him."

Fraser McAlpine, agrees with Austin that it is empowering to see Steve Brookstein persisting with a career he adores. Despite this, Fraser thinks it will be tricky for any ex-winner to fully entangle themselves from the *X Factor* shackles, particularly as, in his pop about-turn, Steve Brookstein is remembered as a notorious contestant, a bounder in the ranks.

"If Steve Brookstein is now doing what he wants to do musically, then more power to him," says Fraser. "But it's likely that *The X Factor* and Steve's subsequent short career borne out of the show will stick in the public's mind rather than any songs he released since. Can you name any of them?

"Steve has every right to be disgruntled about his career after the show. He wasn't even given a second single and had to watch while G4 outsold him in album sales and were seen as the real winners of the show.

"When people talk about it it's about how quickly his *X Factor* career was over and how much better other people have done since. Maybe people will look back on his decisions in years to come and have more respect for him for asserting himself and going it his own way. Maybe they'll think that he wasted a great opportunity at a time it's hard to get music promoted on terrestrial TV or respect for getting a number one single.

"But at the moment, I think it's too fresh in our minds and he's not going to shake that tag of winning *The X Factor* then losing it all so quickly."

Perhaps the problem with Steve's wanting to change direction and score a hit with his own style of music didn't lie with the record label – who wanted to steer him in a direction he wasn't happy with and didn't release his album when he wanted it to be released – but because the acts in the first series of *The X Factor* were so rigidly categorised that the fans he found on the show expected him to continue making the same type of music he sang on the show.

Having sung show numbers or cabaret ditties for four months on telly and simultaneously acquiring fans who like and expect that type of music, it might be difficult to convince people that, actually, your musical preference is death metal and what you really want is to roar along to 'Roots' by Sepultura and bring out albums that align with that genre.

"*Popstars, Fame Academy* and *Pop Idol* might have been on before *The X Factor* but back in the first series, everything was brand new and even the programme makers were finding their feet," says Rowetta Satchell, Steve's fellow competitor. "So once you'd been given a type of music to sing, you had to stick to it. It's different nowadays because they've seen what works and they're much more experimental with music.

"I loved our year and I love the show but in some ways I would love to have been on it later on in the series because they get really top-rate people in to sing with you, and you can sing songs from all different genres and show that you like all sorts of music and can perform different types of songs. But they didn't know that back then and so we were marked out by our genres. In our year it was Steve [who] was a soul singer, Tabby [who] was a rock singer, G4 [who] were opera, so I had to do something else.

"I'd say, 'Can I have a soul song this week please or a rock song?' But the show didn't work like that back then and Simon said you had to stick with those songs and that style of music. They thought it would be easier to market people on the show if they were given a genre and a style and easier for viewers to understand what we were about and support those who sang a style they liked, and it gave us a chance to stand out from one another. Unfortunately that sets you up when you leave the show and it's hard to shake that genre even if you are more at home with different styles.

"I sang 'Over The Rainbow' once on the show. I don't mind the song but I don't really want to have to sing it for the rest of my life. When I came out of *The X Factor,* 'Over The Rainbow' and those type of songs were the songs I had to sing in gigs because that's what the people who saw me on the show expect to hear.

"Sometimes now when I am doing gigs for people who'll know me from the show and have supported me from back in *The X Factor,* I'll do those songs for them because it's not fair on them to do something completely different when they'll expect a certain kind of set. That doesn't mean they're the only songs I can do but *The X Factor* is just one part of my career – which I'm really proud of – and in another area, I might sing more rockier numbers or house music.

"I've been lucky with it all in that the people who know me from Happy Mondays probably didn't follow me on *X Factor* and the people who work on my house music might not know about my time in the Happy Mondays."

Quite the musical chameleon, Rowetta said she did an album specifically for the fans who voted for her during the programme. "I've been able to do all sorts of music but I've also done an *X Factor* album, which is my name for the one you bring out after you've been on the show, which is based on songs you performed on the show and brought out quickly after you leave the show," she says. "You do it because your fans who voted for you week after week listened to those songs and liked your versions of them and so you bring out that type of album for them because you can go back and do other music any time, but that album was right for that part of your career."

Steve may not have thought much of his '*X Factor* album' or his time immediately after the show but HMV head of press, Gennaro Castaldo, also believes that some of Steve's misfortune can be attributed to the fact that it was the first series and everything was up in the air. "It's easy to look at *The X Factor* now and understand all about how it works and what type of people do well on it," says Gennaro. "But back in the first series when Steve Brookstein appeared, *The X Factor* wasn't the omnipresent, all-consuming, all-powerful TV show that it is now.

"Steve was like a fish out of water when he left the show and, to some extent, even during it. He was older, he had his own ideas about his career when a lot of contestants are just starting out and want all the advice they can get, especially from people who are top level in the music industry and have managed artists that they look up to.

"The problem with Steve Brookstein was that when he was on the show, he was presented as a soul singer who wanted to release soul songs. But when he brought out his single, it was pop. There's nothing wrong with that and it's quite conceivable that someone who likes soul music may also like pop music but all the people who've voted for him on the show are getting a different artist almost. It's as if the show makers and the artists themselves didn't know what direction to take and what to do once the series ended and he won.

"That never happened with JLS, Leona Lewis, Alexandra Burke or Girls Aloud. Right from the start, viewers knew what type of artists they were and so they could vote according to whether they liked that type of music among other things. When those acts brought out music, it was the type of music people expected them to bring out and so they didn't grow bored of them or look elsewhere for someone who could sing the type of music they wanted.

"Steve perhaps wasn't packaged in a way that matched his music thereafter. Whether that was down to Steve or the record company is anyone's guess.

"If Steve had appeared in series three or four, he might have found more success because they would have hopefully found out what worked with previous winners and they might have known better how to take him seamlessly from the TV show into the charts. Also, again this is said with hindsight and knowledge of how the other series have panned out – which is a luxury the people in the first series didn't have – Steve Brookstein might have better understood what type of music winners go on to record. Similarly, producers might have been able to see which artists work well in the charts – although that's anyone's guess really – as well as on the show, In that case, he might have decided that it wouldn't have been right for him or he would have had more understanding of the career laid out for him as an *X Factor* contestant and winner.

"That said, I think the fortunate thing with Steve was that if he had been on any other series, he wouldn't have won because they knew what they wanted by that point and were attracting an altogether different type of performer. But that's the paradox. The truth is that Steve Brookstein probably wouldn't have done so well in the show in another year because he wouldn't have been quite right for what *The X Factor* is about now."

Another aspect of Steve Brookstein's career possibly explains why he didn't do as well as G4 or Rowetta. The market for straight-up male solo singers hasn't been as buoyant as, say, R&B performers or bands for some years now. We're pretty tired of men singing cloying ballads, all wearing Topman suits and jaunty hats, doing the same winks to camera and waves to mum at home.

Unwittingly then, the male solo acts are at a disadvantage when they come out of talent TV shows. We might like them on the telly, but when they're out and trying to shift music it's game over lads. In the charts we're championing an altogether different type of pop star.

"Male singers aren't doing so well out of talent TV shows because the market for them as a whole isn't as strong as it has been," says Gennaro Castaldo. "Apart from strong performers like Robbie Williams, Will Young and James Morrison, all of whom have found consistent success and have retained fans regardless of the direction they've taken, the charts are dominated by bands, R&B and female solo artists. Unfortunately for male singers, they don't really have a look in at the moment. That could all change, and it does change because that's how the charts work, but currently that's how things have shaped out and it's unlikely that a male singer would find as much success as a female singer or a band as things are."

If that's not enough, our male singers aren't being hawked in an effective way to us on the screen. On TV, they might come across as likeable and might have enough about them to make us want to vote for them week after week, but being lumped with a sappy song to cover just isn't going to cut it in the charts because there are plenty of other mawkish songs that work a lot better or have been covered in a more enthralling fashion.

"Shows like *The X Factor, Fame Academy* and *Pop Idol* don't spend the time and money finding out what will work for male singers. They're just pumped out every year with identikit careers," says Fraser McAlpine. "Strangely enough, I'm counting Michelle McManus in this category as well because that's how they marketed her too, using a male solo singer prototype.

"These shows use a model Westlife used five years ago and even then it was old. Wearing a smart suit, singing Barry Manilow ballads on a stool and saying your mum is your best friend just doesn't cut it with pop music fans. And by the time the model was given to Steve Brookstein or Leon Jackson even later on, it was out of date."

Male performers may have been given a raw deal because they don't come across as dramatically as Lady Gaga or Pixie-me-face singing their Mariah Carey cover in an off-the-peg suit.

The charts being that odd place where a giant wobbling pink clod called Mr Blobby could flourish over Take That and metal thrasher Meat Loaf, then there's hope for Steve yet. Trends come. Trends go. After all, we're not all still listening to nu rave, grime or grindie. Meanwhile, what of Steve's peers who finished below him in the show? Well not long after he said so long to Sony BMG and set about getting his second album out there, his former mentor Simon Cowell would bravely concede that the real winners from the first series were former buskers turned 'popera' favourites G4, who were mentored by panel pal and show-time sparring partner Louis Walsh.

By all rights, the classically trained runners-up should have been sobbing into their cuppas, watching replays of the finale and wailing 'why not me?' in faultless falsetto. Instead, things were pretty peachy.

More than peachy perhaps. They signed a £1.5m contract with the very same Sony BMG, which at that point also had Steve on its roster. Given how their acts are so remarkably different, it's understandable why Sony would want to sign up the gifted G4 but it must have been a blow for Steve Brooksten to see another contestant get more or less the same prize he got even though they didn't win.

In the first week of release, the quartet's debut album, handily named *G4* and niftily produced by Trevor Horn and Brian Rawling, shifted 245,000 copies.

Then G4 did what Steve Brookstein didn't do at Sony: they came back with a second album, traditionally a notorious stumbling block for artists, particularly after a new series of *The X Factor* had started by then and there were fresh contestants let loose. It was called *G4 And Friends*, and it went to number six in the charts.

Even G4's third album together – third! – *Act Three*, which featured a cameo from Boyzone singer Stephen Gately, reached number 21. That's three top 30 albums; not bad for runners-up, especially when the winner had at that point completely fallen off the radar.

Those albums proved that an act that had flourished on the show but not necessarily won could have success long after the series was dead and buried. The albums achieved double platinum, platinum and gold respectively and for three years they maintained a pretty deft position in both the charts and the public's consciousness with live DVDs, five packed-out UK tours, a book, *G4: Our Way*, and even a special performance for the US Ambassador to the UK during which they warbled 'Star Spangled Banner'.

All this came at a time when winner Steve Brookstein was, by his own admission, "depressed". Though good relations evidently existed between Steve and the canticle-loving quartet, watching their career go from strength to strength must have been a bitter pill for Steve to swallow.

Conversely even G4's eventual break-up after three years together seemed more dignified than Steve's split from Sony. The group said they had grown tired of arguing with each other over petty things and felt if they carried on together they would be deceiving fans and their friendships would dissolve. It seemed a natural end to a hugely successful career.

The band went on *GMTV* to announce their split live on air, thus using the same TV channel that gave them a platform to promote their music to tell the same fans that they were calling it a day. It seemed apt. Besides, being so upfront about their differences and reasons for their split removed any negative speculation and left things on a high.

"We would be rowing backstage then have to put on fake smiles for the fans," high tenor Jonathan Ansell told *The Daily Mail* at the time. "We would row over the most niggling little things – one of us not looking smart enough, or not having shaved properly," said his bandmate Ben Thapa. "We did not want to drag on for another couple of years, growing increasingly resentful of each other."

The difference between this and the way, say, Steve Brookstein or Hear'Say ended things is that G4 seemed in control of the way their split was managed. Ailing pop stars have the propensity to linger long after everyone else has shipped off, hoping that by bringing out one more single or by getting dunked on a TV show they might claw back some fans who still have faith in their talents. Sometimes, as we've heard, the market for a particular type of singer might just not be there at the right moment or the music might not be up to scratch and people quite realistically look for other bands and acts. But there's a lot to be said for a band quitting while they're ahead, being upfront about it and doing so on good terms.

Those good terms meant that the band finished their tour commitments and parted as friends. The 'Guildhall 4' may not have been G4 for much longer but the band had achieved a lot in a short time and certainly now, when people talk of the bulging throng of TV contestants, it's hard to imagine them among the ranks of The Cheeky Girls and Chico.

The band members have all retained successful careers within music, radio and television, which, after first appearing on our screens in the early Noughties, is no easy feat.

After leaving the group, Bognor-born Jonathan Ansell was

approached by four major record labels for a solo deal. He eventually signed with Universal Music Group and his album, *Tenor At The Movies*, went to number one in the Classical Chart, staying there for three weeks. *Tenor At The Movies* also notched up a number nine spot in the official charts, adding another stripe to Jonathan's sleeve. Consequently, his entry made him the youngest tenor to go to the top of the Classical Charts.

Baritone Mike Christie, who if you squint carefully enough you can just about make out as a rosy-cheeked chorister in Hugh Grant mush-fest *Four Weddings And A Funeral*, is writing an opera based on his own life story as well as releasing an album of original songs. He's even famous enough to have appeared on *Blue Peter* and *Through The Keyhole*. Grimsby-born G4-er Matthew Stiff took up a presenting spot on ClassicFM and has allegedly gone back to his studies, while tenor Ben Thapa has released his own solo album, *Songs Of My Childhood*, and still performs around the country.

"G4 had a unique selling point," says Gennaro Castaldo. "They were opera singers in a pop competition. The official charts aren't generally awash with opera singers or people who perform classical music so there was more room for them in the charts. They were unusual and interesting for what people had previously seen on TV shows like *The X Factor*."

Mancunian Rowetta Satchell, who finished fourth in the first series of *The X Factor,* had worked as a singer for the Happy Mondays for 10 years and even supported Oasis at Wembley before entering the show, and had her own recording contract. But Rowetta, who looks back fondly on her time on the first series of *The X Factor*, still believes that a big chunk of her success in current years can be pinned down to the show. Rather than get lippy about not having a spin-off show, annex in Simon Cowell's house and a room full of £50 notes, Rowetta reckons that contestants shouldn't expect so much from the show beyond seeing it as an opportunity of a lifetime to get their music out there.

"Being in the Mondays and having singing and touring experience helped me enormously because I didn't take *The X Factor* too seriously," says Rowetta. "I turned up drunk to the audition and was probably more light-hearted about the whole thing than others. I did *The X Factor* because I love Simon Cowell and I wanted him to know I could sing.

"It was just a bit of a joke but I got so much out of it that I didn't really expect from being in the show. Even now, I am still recognised from doing the show. It's five years ago and people always ask, 'Who else was in your group with Steve? And who was that woman called Verity and who was that Irish woman?' But I think because I'd had a singing career with the Mondays, people might have already known me but *The X Factor* made my music available to a whole new audience who might not have known anything of the Mondays or my time with them."

Rowetta, who has a weekly radio show, regular gigs and is the voice sampled on Black Eyed Peas' 2009 hit 'Boom Boom Pow', thinks in some respects it is easier for runners-up to blossom because there's not the burden to succeed immediately and retain that success that comes with winning. "I don't think I had the pressure of people who do win because people don't expect too much of you," she says.

"People are always pleased when they hear what I'm doing and often they'll stop me in the supermarket and want to know what I'm up to but it's not pushed down people's throats how well or not you're doing. You just get on with doing it and if they want to be interested in your career they can be, but your every career move isn't splashed over every paper going.

"You're not overexposed. People come and find you on Facebook and websites because they're interested in you. I've been on telly a bit but I don't have a PR machine where I've got to do this and that. I get to do what's relevant to me so when people do see you, they're pleased to see you.

Rowetta's positive experience on the programme has made her critical of those who moan about it to curry favour with the press or to get themselves back in the spotlight. "I don't do every *X Factor* programme going," she says. "A lot of people who've been on the show have to be seen all the time even though many of them are negative about *The X Factor* in the press. I don't think it's cool to be negative about *The X Factor* and if you do too many of these shows and interviews you end up saying 'I like this one and that one and I didn't think they were good last week' about current contestants and I wouldn't want to do that.

"I talk about it every week on my radio show when the series starts but I try not to be critical. In my opinion, the show gives us a really, really good launch of our careers if you haven't already had one and a boost if you have. That's how it should be seen. A lot of people forget that people hadn't heard of most of these contestants before they went on *The X Factor.* A lot of people hadn't heard of me so I'm very grateful and respectful of the show and any new contestants who go on it."

Rowetta believes that too many contestants feel let down by Simon Cowell for not signing them after leaving the show and lay any future career blips on him and his apparent lack of interest in their subsequent careers. "I know a lot of people feel they've had a bad time of it because they don't work with Simon afterwards. Well I don't work with Simon and yet I was one of his favourites. I'm not bitter at all, and this is serious, but I got a lot from doing that show and I don't think people should feel entitled to work with Simon just because they've been on *The X Factor.*

"Not all of my jobs since have come from *The X Factor* but I still put a lot down to the show and some of the people who book me do so because they saw me on the show. The only bad thing is when I'm tired I need a day off, but then you think what was I doing before *The X Factor*? I wasn't doing a lot so I'm really grateful."

Rowetta also appeared on a Living TV show, *Rehab*, to help with her alcoholism, and sees herself as having two separate careers since leaving *The X Factor*: her *X Factor* career and another that's entirely different from that, but that they've each helped one another and have kept her busy and doing something she loves.

"A lot of my dance music isn't through *The X Factor*," she says. "Not so long ago I promoted my dance single with a DJ who wouldn't know about *The X Factor* but the following day I did a gig I wouldn't have got if it weren't for me going on *The X Factor*.

"The Freemasons recently played one of my tunes, which is nothing to do with me being an *X Factor* contestant, and the Black Eyed Peas have just sampled me on 'Boom Boom Pow', which is massive but not to do with *The X Factor*. There are two professional sides to me. I don't really talk about *The X Factor* loads but I'll always say that it's really helped with one side of my career. The only reason I don't talk about it loads is because I don't want all of the DJs to know too much about it. I'm not embarrassed but I want them to think of me as a dance singer not someone who sings 'Over The Rainbow' because I don't really do that any more."

Another surprising result of the show is that since Leona Lewis won *The X Factor* in 2006, Rowetta suspects that any sceptics have put their misgivings about the programme to one side and the show as a whole – and the contestants it spawns – have become more credible. As a result, Rowetta thinks Leona's gargantuan achievements have made some otherwise reluctant promoters and agents more amenable to hiring former *X Factor* contestants to perform gigs.

"To begin with, knowing about *The X Factor* put a few DJs off but that's all changed now since Leona Lewis," says Rowetta. "I don't think it was as credible as it has become since. It needed someone to become massively successful and Leona has and I don't think anyone would have minded being a runner-up to Leona.

"I wouldn't have minded. I didn't mind being a runner-up to Steve Brookstein in the first series and I don't think anyone would have minded being a runner-up to Leona.

"People don't talk about the first show so much nowadays or about Steve Brookstein but that's natural when we've had so many subsequent series.

"I don't want to distance myself from *The X Factor* but when I talk about it I talk about the actual show as a whole now and not just about my year because it's become bigger and better anyway and it's become more than what it was when I went on it.

"I think the first year, the producers, judges, executives and us contestants were just learning what to do themselves but it's become bigger. It's a completely different show. Even established acts are fighting to get on there because they know they'll have a number one if they go on the show.

"It's such a great start to your career. It's a great show. It's like *American Idol*. People want to get on the show and mentor the contestants. I would have loved to have sung with George Michael and have a singing lesson with him. People are desperate to be part of it because it's such a brilliant show. I think good on anyone who appears on it as a contestant.

"I wish they'd had the themes and the guests on the first year because when you look back at what it was and what it is now, it makes it look a bit crap in comparison. If you look at the first series and then a more recent one, it was completely different from what it is now. But that's natural."

Rowetta feels strongly about the labelling of runners-up as 'losers' before they've had a shot of cracking the charts and finds the way in which some winners' achievements are dismissed unfair. "A lot of people thought Rhydian Roberts should have won the fourth series but it's not about that," she says. "It is a popularity contest, it's a vote. I never thought, 'Oh I'm a loser.' I hate all that. They're not losers and I'm not a loser, we just weren't as popular as the winner.

"I was the final woman in the series. It didn't mean I was the best woman. It just meant I was the most popular with the judges and the voters, which is great, but I never ever thought I was the best singer in the whole world. I was just popular with those voters at that time, that's all.

"People say to me that I should've won the first series. No, I shouldn't have. I didn't get the most votes, I shouldn't have won. Steve got the most votes. Steve was the most popular act with people watching. He should have won and he did because he was most popular. We shouldn't take that away from him."

Flattering as people voting you in week after week may be, Rowetta thinks some contestants would be wise to keep their feet on the ground and remember that being big-headed about their time on the show isn't going to do them any favours because the real hard work begins once they've been booted out.

"Some people get forgotten about after appearing on the show," she says.

"Others think by going on *The X Factor* they're stars already and they deserve to be treated like stars. They're not and it isn't going to keep them in good stead with those around them.

"I had already been around real stars. At Glastonbury with the Mondays, I was in a room next to David Bowie. He's a proper star and he acted really normal. He didn't have a manager with him. He said he doesn't have one. All he has is a lawyer and a PA. He came around and talked to everyone. He was really pleasant and he's a legend. I just think that it's people like that you should learn from. He had a really good approach to his success.

"Lloyd Daniels from series six said he wanted to go on the show to be recognised in the streets, which I found disappointing. I know he's only a young kid and he might not have realised how that sounded but that's why some people go on *The X Factor*; to be famous and that's really sad. You can be famous for a matter of months but your singing talent should stay with you and that's what I think people should focus on.

"Anything else that comes from your singing and being on the show – great. You can't build a career on wanting fame alone. It has to be because you're talented and want to perform. Singing should be first and foremost and if it isn't, go on another TV show that will allow you to be famous for doing nothing because there's plenty of them about. I know *The X Factor* is about more than just singing but it should start with your singing and because you want people to hear your voice. It's the best way of getting exposure, it's fantastic. That's why you should do the show – if you're a good singer, not because you want people to recognise you on the streets.

"I have had so many opportunities from *The X Factor*. I performed on the Children in Need stage with G4 because we were the only ones that year to have children and so it wasn't the winner who was asked to go on. I was on the stage with Kylie and Katie Price and Peter Andre and with the BBC orchestra when I hadn't won. That was the highlight of my year. Then I was headlining Manchester Pride. And you look at the papers and you're supposed to have flopped and it's just not true... because I'm always working and if I wasn't working I'd always be moaning that I wasn't working and I'd be gutted because I love working and I love what I do."

Rowetta's *X Factor* peer Tabby Callaghan is similarly reflective about his time on the show. Tabby, who is from Sligo in Ireland, was a rock fan who originally auditioned with a band he'd been playing with for years. He was encouraged to come back by himself and quickly won over the judges.

After leaving the show with a respectable third place rosette, Tabby worked with songwriter Mark Hudson, toured the country and is now releasing a new album. Having been exposed to fame after leaving *The X Factor* and not enjoying the level of fanfare, Tabby says he's determined to make his music career a success the old way, by working away at his music and winning over fans with the songs instead of trading in on his *X Factor* fame.

Believing that there's little time to deal the *X Factor* card once the show's over, Tabby reckons it's better to accept that there may not be provisions in place for runners-up and to seek a career on your own terms rather than chase the *X Factor* dream. "*The X Factor* is like an alchemy," he says. "You go on it trying to make something brilliant out of something good or not so good. But I also think that *The X Factor* is a machine and when it's done with you it spits you out. No one questions what happens to all these winners who come out and then are dropped a year later. They don't go to an *X Factor* retirement home. They just fade away and people move on.

"It is a TV show. A music show with 10 minutes of music and the rest is drama. It's an entertainment show and that's what it does, it entertains even if it means the music element is only small. And when you go on the show, you are doing telly sales really. You go on there as a salesperson selling your music to people. That's what it is. But you can't deny that it's great exposure. Millions of people watch that show every week and you're not going to get that coverage on any other TV show. It's the biggest TV show in the UK so you may be telly sales but at least you're doing it to the biggest possible audience.

"But by the time you have a contract and are working on material, it's the turn of the next year's contestants and the focus goes on them. That's the nature of the show and that's what difficult about it afterwards."

Tabby also didn't expect there to be such a huge emphasis on being a celebrity once he had left the show and says he turned away from that aspect even if it meant that he had less exposure thereafter. "The whole celebrity aspect is pretentious and I didn't bargain for it," he says. "That's not what I went in *The X Factor* for and I don't bother with it. I could quite easily have got swept along and gone to any cheese and wine party going and hobnobbed with people whom I'd never meet again but I didn't bother with it.

"Instead, I toured constantly for two years but then I got to a point where I didn't want to any more and I had a period of being depressed. It wasn't a particularly nice state to be in but now I'm in a good place and things have turned around. I'm writing music that I care about and people like it."

Despite not enjoying the unwanted celebrity aspect that appearing on the show brought with it, Tabby appreciates the level of exposure being on *The X Factor* gave him. "The show helps to put you and your music out there and makes you well-known but it's how you handle the fame and the choices you're offered afterwards that matters. I chose to do things my way. I put some songs on MySpace recently. Three thousand people had listened to one song in a day and 300,000 people have listened to it now.

"It might take longer to do things that way but I'm really happy with the material I've been writing and I'm happy with the support I've been given from people listening to that music."

But people haven't always been so accepting of Tabby and the singer admits that there were occasions when he was looked down on for being a contestant on the show, almost to the extent where people expect his music to be trite and deriding him before he plays a single note. Even so, he concedes that victory is all the sweeter when disbelievers acknowledge his talent.

"*The X Factor* nowadays is all about people who've been on crutches or come from the wrong side of town," he says. "You can play that up and hope to win votes that way but in the long term you need to rely on your musical talent if you want to make it as a singer. I've been trying to win people over one by one ever since I went on *The X Factor.*

"I played a show at the Cavern Club in Liverpool and it was packed to the rafters and I remember seeing three journalist types at the back, arms crossed turning their noses down at me, ready to completely write me off and just being really snobby about me because I'd been on the show. After the gig, one of them came up to me and said I'd blown him away. It felt so good to have him realise that. Now I'm doing things my way with my career."

Unlike Rowetta, Tabby says that he would have liked more support from *The X Factor* after leaving the show but is now pretty happy with his lot. "I'd be lying if I said I got exactly what I wanted out of *The X Factor.* I wish I hadn't trusted people so much afterwards in the sense that I wish I'd had more support once the show was over but you learn from it. And now I've got a career I'm happy with and that's important to me. I'm making music for a living and that's great.

"I'll still say that going on *The X Factor* is a great experience for learning about the music business and it is a business, the music is only a tiny part of it. There's no right or wrong way of dealing with life after *The X Factor* and the choices you're offered or even in the music industry as a whole but it's a very good taster of what it is like to try and succeed in that industry. If you want to pursue music, then going on *The X Factor* is a good way of seeing how things work and what you're in for.

"One thing I've found out from doing the show is that you either become someone who accepts what's laid out in front of you while you can and says yes to everyone and everything and do all the tours and wear all the suits and be clean cut or you say no, not for me. The bland will say yes always and will just do what they're told and that's fine. They might get further with the show because they're more malleable; in fact those people almost always win because of that. There's a place for both types of people but I'm not like that.

"Nowadays, you know what type of singers they want now from that show – or at least which are popular with viewers – and in some ways it's easier to see whether you are that type of singer and whether it would be worth your time applying.

"So I would say that I've learned a lot from doing the show and one of the things I know is that I'm not one of those people who will just say yes. But that is also fine. There's room in the charts for different types of performers with entirely different outlooks. Otherwise it would be a very dull show – and it is an entertainment show so it needs to have different types of performers – but more importantly, music would be incredibly dull if everyone thought the same."

Forewarned is forearmed but in the case of the contestants from the first series and those who appeared thereafter, they didn't really have that much inkling of how the show would pan out and what a successful format it would go on to be.

Even with the first series being more of a free-for-all in terms of the variety of performers who got through to the final, it would appear that most contestants have by and large gained something positive from being on *The X Factor*. Maybe their differences in style – hello rock, opera, pop and soul, there's room for you here – meant that afterwards they didn't immediately have to compete against each other for work, nor would they have the level of expectation that people now have of contestants who go on the programme, be it to fall on their faces at the first hurdle or go on to be mega successful.

Likewise, it would seem that each of the acts from the first series is now working on music that they have always wanted to record. *The X Factor* launched them, they did a few lucrative gigs they perhaps didn't have their hearts in but now they've been able to focus on their own sounds a little more. Fair play.

Perhaps then, much of the hoo-haa surrounding Steve Brookstein's brief foray into the charts could be pinned down to *The X Factor* being a new show that didn't yet know what to do with its performers or its performers didn't know what to do with the prize they'd been handed. It's easy to look by on the sidelines with the gift of hindsight or no personal attachment but perhaps looking back, they were all just finding their feet and too much was expected of what is really just a family entertainment show, no matter how much contestants expect from appearing on it.

As it is, it seems churlish to land the blame solely at the feet of Simon Cowell. Yes he wants to make money and work with acts who are credible and talented. But then if he didn't, he wouldn't be much of a music executive would he? If he and the label were pulling one way and Steve Brookstein was pulling the other, the ship isn't going to move. Shooting a few barbed comments back and forth won't dent the show's appeal or put people off applying.

# Chapter 7

# *The X Factor* **Series Two**

Justin Timberlake must have thanked his lucky stars when former New Look shop assistant turned *X Factor* winner Shayne Ward started rocking trilby hats, leather jackets and sharp dance moves and gave him the inspiration for a whole new image to take to the charts. Thank you Mr Ward.

"Justin Timberlake is the model they try with male singers in *The X Factor* if the Westlife one doesn't fit," says Fraser McAlpine. They did it with Shayne Ward and even Lloyd Daniels in series six, at least five years after it was popular.

"Well Justin Timberlake hasn't changed his sound in years. He was really popular back at the start of the Noughties and yet they still bring out male singers based on that model. They know he was popular and edgier than the Westlife template so they use him as a model. Put the singer in a leather jacket and a hat, give him some faux Michael Jackson dance moves and they think it'll work. That's what they did for Shayne Ward."

Back in 2005, the victory crown was all Shayne's for the keeping – even if it did mean aping JT for all he was worth – and Steve Brookstein was but a distant memory in *The X Factor's* history. A good-looking, amiable chap who was styled to within an inch of his life to resemble man of that moment Timberlake, Shayne beat off peers Andy Abraham – the bin man from the telly! – and brothers Journey South.

For a winner, Shayne has gone on to have a fruitful career. He's had a number one and a number two album and was even considered by Gary Barlow as a replacement for Jason Orange when he threatened to quit Take That.

Even so Shayne, who is working on his third album, remains realistic about fame. "I remember having this talk with Leon Jackson, who unfortunately got dropped. Once you've won the show, you know that there is going to be another show straight away and that all the focus from the public is going to be on the new show," Shayne told *Manchester Evening News.* "That's why you have to use your time to prove why the people voted for you.

"I've done that now with two successful albums and two tours. And the third album is 100 per cent unbelievable. It's going to be coming out."

That remains to be seen but certainly a five-year career and two albums to his name is quite an achievement when there are so many reality TV winners around.

# Chapter 8

# *The X Factor* Series Three

Hackney lass Leona Lewis is the *X Factor* quality seal of approval in a sea of soft releases. Before she entered the show in 2006, the most contestants could hope for was a spread in a weekly celebrity magazine about how they really fancied Simon Cowell or Sharon Osbourne or Louis Walsh and a couple of karaoke covers. Leona changed everything. Or, as series one contestant Rowetta Satchell puts it: "Simon was talking about giving *The X Factor* up before Leona Lewis came along because it was getting like *Pop Idol* where they'd got good contestants and put them in the UK charts but they were like, what do we do now? How do we take the show to the next level? But Leona Lewis transformed it. She's world class and internationally successful."

Even with good competition in the face of runner-up Ben Mills and grans' favourite Ray Quinn, she still stood a world apart from anything ever seen on UK talent searches. Noting this quality, those around her released a courtesy single in 'A Moment Like This' – itself a cover of *American Idol* winner Kelly Clarkson's song, which is a further example of the reality TV snake eating its own tail – and then took a year in America – America! – to make her cool and credible whatever that means. Well whatever it means, it worked.

"The show was entirely caught out by Leona's actual talent," says Fraser McAlpine. "Before she won, no one ever sustained a career, and they weren't expected to. Since then, they had Alexandra Burke, and she did well because they could flog the idea that they find talent like Leona Lewis – so they work on templates.

"Leona can really sing, so she's freakish in that context [and] that's why she succeeded. The other winners were simply the people who won a TV show. They were all David Sneddons."

So the show was caught out by talent. It wasn't a personality contest, says celebrity writer Mr Holy Moly. The thing that stood out about Leona was exactly what the judges had been banging on about all these years – *The X Factor* itself. "Leona Lewis is incredibly successful but she is boring. It goes to show that people don't actually want or care if she comes on stage dressed as a clown and has fireworks in the background," he says. "People don't need that… they're just looking for substance."

Leona is substance herself, being nominated for Grammys, Brits, named as *Billboard* magazine's top new artist and the world's sexiest vegetarian alongside Anthony Kiedis. Didn't she do well.

There is little point in denying that *The X Factor* has helped bring Leona Lewis to the attention of the public. Sure, someone as talented as LL might have found fame eventually but she didn't and her existence in the charts across the world is testament to the show's success. While this is all la–de–dah, let's move onto the other side of the *X Factor* coin: Leona's successor, Leon Jackson.

# Chapter 9

# *The X Factor* **Series Four**

Instead of going to college and spending three years attending lectures about existential philosophy, Leon Jackson deferred his entry to Napier University and spent the latter stages of his teens singing duets with Kylie Minogue wearing a Kylie-length lacy body stocking on national TV, winning series four of *The X Factor*, appearing on stage with his hero Michael Bublé and scoring a number one single in the UK and Ireland with 'When You Believe'. On the face of things, there could have been worse ways for him to spend his salad days.

Unlike his contemporaries who might lose their first jobs after a preliminary period or who might go on to do something else with their lives without scrutiny, Leon, who had never performed in public in the year before his *X Factor* win, was to be seen as someone whose career had gone off the radar within a year of his appearance on the ITV programme.

The reason for this was that the young West Lothian chap landed a contract with Sony BMG as part of the prize for winning the fourth series of *The X Factor* but parted company with the label just over a year later. Runner-up Rhydian Roberts, however, scooped higher album sales than Leon but remained gracious about Leon's career.

"In fairness, none of it was his fault – I don't think he expected to win," Rhydian told *The Guardian*. "But he can hold his head high. He had a taste of fame and a number one single at a very young age. The only qualm I have about coming second – and this is the truth – is that perhaps if I'd won I would have had more worldwide exposure, maybe gone on Oprah."

Many people saw Leon, the quiet, modest singer who never mentioned any desire to cosy up on Oprah Winfrey's sofa, as the underdog in the *X Factor* race and expected opera-singing Rhydian Roberts, like Leon also mentored by Dannii Minogue, or pop brother and sister Same Difference to take the title. In style and outlook, Same Difference and Rhydian were both unlike any other act to be tipped to win the programme. But they didn't win. Instead it was to be Leon's night of glory and rightly so, according to ex-contestant Rowetta Satchell.

"Anyone who wins *The X Factor* deserves it," says Rowetta. "They were the most popular with viewers at that time and so they should have won because they were the one with the most viewers behind them and had the most votes to win. That's how it should be. It was fair that Steve Brookstein won in my year because he was the most popular with people and it's fair with any of the contestants who get the most votes in the final. Leon Jackson deserved to win. Whatever anyone says afterwards about other contestants who should have won, it was the winner who was most popular in the final and they deserve their glory."

Glory was Leon's for a while and, indeed, even His Royal Simonness, who'd been supportive when Leon Jackson won the show and seems to remain appreciative of his talents and accomplishments, bit his tongue and told only *The Times* that he thought Rhydian should have won the show once things went slightly awry for the young singer. "I know I'm not supposed to say Rhydian should have won but it's true. I believe that 100%," said Simon.

Even so, Leon took being dropped by his label and management in his stride and said, with timely wisdom beyond his years, that he understood that the music industry was quick-moving and that even the best of artists could switch record labels or go it independently during their career.

What he could take from it all was that his debut album, *Right Now*, had reached number four in the charts and he'd made an appearance on the first of the live showdowns in series five of *The X Factor* – but now it was time to move on to other things. As pop foundations go, he had had some pretty impressive grounding in a very short space of time. "I had a great year and learned so much recording and releasing my album," Leon said on his MySpace page. "Every artist knows these things can go either way. I'm really look-ing forward to my tour and doing more writing."

Like many winners before him who'd been taken off the man-agement books within a year, or sooner than expected, Leon was marred with the 'flopstar' tag. Rowetta believes it is unfair to brand the young singer so.

Rather than playing down Leon's achievements and assuming that he failed because he left the label to which he signed after his win, Rowetta says we should acknowledge his accomplishments and bear in mind that he has a long time ahead of him to build his career in a way that suits him. As rungs on a ladder go, his win was, after all, pretty nifty. "People are too harsh on Leon Jackson," says Rowetta. "He's just a kid. He's what... 20? He's got his whole career ahead of him to do whatever he likes. It's not over for him yet just because he's not with the management he signed to when he won *The X Factor* or just because he hasn't released a song for a while.

"Do you know what? That kid has already had a number one sin-gle and he's got the rest of his life to build on that success and make more albums if he wants to. So what if he's not with the same record label or if he doesn't get another number one single immediately. That's the music business, that's what happens; people change labels and people don't always get number one singles and albums no mat-ter how famous or talented they are.

"People should see it as a great first step for him in his career. He can do whatever he likes now he's had that great starting place on

*The X Factor* and in the charts. How many people can say they've won *The X Factor* and had a number one single afterwards? Especially at his age. He's done really well.

"So many people want to win *The X Factor* and he's done it. We should think more of his achievements and his future and less of the fact that he's left the label. He can still work in the music industry even if he isn't with that label, it just might mean that it will take him longer to get a single together. So what? He still has his talent, he can still do it.

"That's just how the music industry works; you're with a label and then you're dropped. It happens all the time but still he has lots of experience in the industry now and he's had some of the best people in the business helping him and giving him feedback on *The X Factor*."

Singer Daniel DeBourg appeared on the same series as Leon. Daniel, who had previously written 'Money', which got to number five in the charts for Brummie superstar Jamelia, has gone on to have success with DJ Ironik and the dance market as well writing for fellow *X Factor* contestants. Likewise, he thinks that Leon's career shouldn't be written off so easily given his age and that the demand for contestants is always going to be affected by the constant influx of new acts and singers pumped out annually. "Leon is such a talented boy. He deserved to win and I really think that he will come back and become really successful," says Daniel.

Daniel, whose song was sampled on R&B singer Bobby Valentine's album before he went on *The X Factor*, is also acutely aware of the high turnover of singers from *The X Factor*. There can only be so much of a swell of *X Factor* contestants before people get bored and move over to the next on the production line.

Knowing this, Daniel always tried to steer away from relying too heavily on the programme, and instead thought of it as an excellent way to bring attention to his talents rather than take it for granted that he'd get a recording deal and all the trimmings as a result of being on the show; or just going down *The X Factor* career path for the sake of staying in the public eye, which for him would have been the wrong reason to enter the competition in the first place.

"The problem is that the nature of the show means that once you've done yout thing, the management and label have someone else to worry about, another contestant or winner and then they become a priority and so have less time and money to spend on you and getting your music out there because everyone's interested in the latest sensation and everyone wants to hear their first single and album," says Daniel.

"Fans move on to the next winner and the new batch of contestants and they are soon the ones in the papers, so the previous year's winner gets pushed aside to make room for them. That's just the way the show is, by its very nature it needs to find fresh talent and new contestants and that means investing in them as soon as they've won the show. So once all the interest and attention from the label dries up and fans move on to the next winner, you're on your own.

"That's why I didn't really try to trade on *The X Factor* too much and once I could, I signed with Warners and started working behind the scenes and going back underground because that's where I was happiest. I never expected too much of the programme and it's worked out well for me. I enjoyed it but I always saw it as a vehicle for getting my music out there, which is why I wasn't so fussed that I wasn't on the tour and everything afterwards.

"Going underground suited me and I never expected that the show would change everything for me, just that it would give my music exposure to new people. You can't expect Simon Cowell and the judges to be with you after you've finished the show just as you can't expect that you'll get a number one album just from appearing on it.

"But I think it's harder on those who don't have as much of an understanding of how it works or who get signed to the same label afterwards. It can work out fine for them but for me, I wanted to go my own way and get away from it all. There's more freedom when you go it alone and you're not then competing with the same people you were in the show with.

"However, I do think that Leon has the talent and the personality to bounce back. He has everything going for him and he has got a lot of success under his belt but he might just need the time to go underground and work out a direction that works for him and find a label interested in that.

"If he does that, I think he has every chance of making it work for him and coming back with more success than before. It's always going to be difficult for winners because they will always be compared to other winners and with their early success. But he can do it and I think he will do it."

Austin Drage, a contestant in the fifth series of *The X Factor* the year after Leon won, also thinks that winning can be irksome for singers because it can be harder for them to carve their own path. As a result, they can become disillusioned with the industry quickly because it isn't how they expect it to be. Austin is still performing with a band and writing, recording and playing music.

Having seen winners forgotten quickly, Austin thinks it's a shame that Leon is no longer in the public eye and that he has been written off so quickly. But that is a paradox only a winner will have; they will get all the rewards and attention to begin with but if they don't recapture that, they're a failure. "Winning is a double-edged sword," says Austin. "If you finish first, you could be pushed in a direction of singing a song that you love, the label love, the public love and it can go that way and you're a big success and it can all happen for you. Plus, you've won the show and you have all that exposure that comes with it.

"But on the other hand, look at Leon Jackson. He won *The X Factor* and now no one knows who he is. It's a shame because he's a good guy and he's got a good little voice but he could walk past you in the street and you probably wouldn't know who he was and you wouldn't think he'd won the show or what series he won.

"That's just how it goes sometimes. It's not his fault, it's just the way things are. You go in a direction that isn't quite right, people don't like it as much as they're expected to and then you're forgotten about and the next winner or runner-up comes along and people are more interested in them and it starts again."

Daniel DeBourg is another who believes that the *X Factor* brand can be a hindrance to singers once they're in the charts and that it's often better to put the *X Factor* tag to one side and focus on becoming known for musical output than having appeared on the programme, which, as we've seen, can be ancient history once a new series starts up again. *X Factor* contestant? What *X Factor* contestant?

Daniel found that sometimes people in the industry would have been sceptical of his talents if they knew he'd been on *The X Factor*. Knowing this, they might just expect him to be a certain type of performer – the ballads and suits style – just because of his appearance on the fourth series. It can be an albatross around the neck of any singer if they allow the programme to dictate their career afterwards rather than take hold of it and shape it in a way that suits them.

By starting afresh, like a new performer, Daniel thinks there's less pressure to do everything; have multiple number one albums, pop up on Madonna's next single, sing for Nelson Mandela and chum up to Simon Cowell at his birthday parties. It's all a bit more simple. But of course, as with many things, that is easier said than done, especially for a winner who will always have that tag hanging over them.

*"The X Factor* has been great for me," says Daniel. "One producer saw me on the show and called me up and worked with me because they'd seen me on the programme. I wouldn't have got that work or that exposure to those people otherwise. That's why the show is so great; it puts you under people's noses and gives you greater opportunity to work in music and that itself is priceless because it can be hard to get known out there when so many people want to do the same thing as you. So for that, I will always be glad I did the show.

"But I do think that if I had gone to the live *X Factor* shows and done the *X Factor*-esque album afterwards and if I had finished higher up than I did, then I would have eventually seen the show as a hindrance because I wouldn't have had the control that I now have over my career, which is important to me.

"I would have had to focus on *The X Factor* and not had that time to work out which projects to work on and which would suit me best. It would have been harder for me to step away from the show and not get tarred with the same brush as everyone else and I think it would have turned people against working with me because they might not expect me to have an idea of what I want to do.

"The other thing is that while it's absolutely fine to sing covers on TV and even during the tour, it can be hard to get away from that and away from being associated with those songs that you sing. I knew that singing 'Build Me Up Buttercup' wasn't right for me in the long term but I think it's quite easy to become pigeonholed or forgotten if you carry on doing covers rather than work on your own material. You then become written off as someone who has no idea about music."

Many fans of Daniel's music haven't the foggiest idea that he was once a contestant on *The X Factor* and he thinks that if Leon manages to find a way for his music to be the focus, rather than his win on the show, then he has a good chance to make it again and escape the shackles of the expectation. "I went underground almost after coming out of the show and went back to working on music and writing, which is something I always loved doing," he says. "But good things have come from doing the show for me and I have total respect for Simon Cowell. I think he's a very shrewd and knowledgeable man.

"Going underground was a natural step for me because I wasn't the type of artist who wanted to sing 'Build Me Up Buttercup' as I had in my final week. I knew that that music wasn't for me and I knew the type of music that I did want to work on and got on with doing that.

"Obviously, that doesn't always work for other singers who are quite happy to sing those types of songs but I do think that getting away from *The X Factor* can help you have a longer career or at least give you a career that you have more control over in the long run."

Daniel, who was mentored by Louis Walsh on the programme, never watched any of the previous series of *The X Factor* and knows that being an ex-contestant of the show isn't something that is likely to impress those who now listen to his music. Even worse, some people view *The X Factor* as good reason to harbour low expectations of any singer beyond the same, tired, old numbers, and that any success they have is a direct result of the programme and has nothing to do with good old-fashioned graft and talent.

"I never used to watch *The X Factor* before I entered the show," says Daniel. "I think a lot of people who like my music would probably never watch it or think of me being on the show because it's just not their scene and they wouldn't imagine that someone who records music that I do would be interested in it.

"There's nothing wrong with *The X Factor*, it's a great show and I'm glad I was a part of it but the music on the show is very different from the genres I'm interested in. Our tracks are on the *Twice As Nice* albums and they're big in Ibiza, which is a scene far removed from *The X Factor*. They just wouldn't look to the programme for the latest Ibiza dance act because the show doesn't usually attract those types of singers.

"Sometimes I think if people knew I had been a contestant on *The X Factor,* they'd think my success came directly from the show, which can hold you back and keep you lower in people's estimations even if you've done it all off your own back, written your own songs and worked hard in the industry before going on *The X Factor*. As it happens, it makes any success that you have that bit sweeter. It means that if you do do well it's not just because they've seen you on telly. I think you get more respect from people that way."

Series five contestant Daniel Evans also feels he was judged harshly after leaving the programme and that it can leave an indelible stain on your pop career.

"I do think you can be judged unfairly after leaving the programme," he says.

"I had some bad comments from two very influential people and people remember that. What they don't know is the unbelievable pressure there is, coping with songs you do not choose, dodgy makeovers, dance routines you hate – I can't dance! – and all the different cameras that fly around you [and you] have to find them at different parts of the songs.

"If you go out early but have good comments it's better than staying longer but with bad comments. It's all very good upping votes and ratings by being nasty, but after it's all finished and they go back to their record companies and management companies, people like me struggle to get work on the back of those comments.

"I know 'real' musicians do not take *X Factor* artists seriously unless they absolutely prove themselves as stars. They see it as all manufactured but to be honest – and I'm a musician, I play keys and write music – I think they are just jealous and would love to have that kind of publicity!"

Quite. The other Daniel, Daniel Debourg thinks that part of the issues winners have sustaining interest is down to the music released after they leave *The X Factor*, which is often fairly pedestrian, chosen so that any contestant could use it and not sound terrible. But this can mean that fans have no real sense of what the singer can do. It's only if the act is then dropped that the winner has a chance to perform something a bit more in their style and, by that point, they might be written off as yesterday's chip paper.

"The problem is that the music that is released by the winners isn't always the best and isn't always the stuff that is going to suit them," said Daniel DeBourg.

"It's kind of one size fits all because they have to get it ready and malleable for all the finalists and they don't have so long to work on it afterwards because they want to strike while the iron's hot and get the song out in the shortest time possible. That makes business sense and it probably makes sense to viewers who've spent four months watching your progress and want to hear the fruits of your labour but sometimes it means that a quick release is favoured over working on great songs, which is what will help artists sustain a career and keep them distinct from every other singer going.

"If you don't move away from doing these generic songs or spend time afterwards getting some tracks together that are tailored for you, then you end up with a pretty indistinct sound. People may get bored of that quite quickly, which is where it sometimes goes a little wrong because they move on to the next winner or the next contestant and then you're gone.

"That didn't happen with Leona or with Will Young and look where they are. They were both really talented performers anyway but that has been enhanced by brilliant songs that they went away and spent time working on and making them fit them rather than the other way around. They've become respected in their own rights and have really found a sound that works and which moves with the times.

"When it goes wrong it's usually because they haven't had enough time to work on songs or they haven't worked out exactly what type of singer they're going to be and so have these one size fits all songs that easily tail off.

"I really do think that if Leon had the right songs he could turn it all around and become really big. I think he just needs a bit of time to work out where he wants to go with his music and how to do that but he's got the rest of his life to figure that out. His career isn't finished just because of one setback and nor does it mean that he has lost his talent. Plus, people really like him or they wouldn't have voted him as the winner of the series so hopefully he'll still have those people on board and willing to listen to anything new that he brings out and also be able to draw in some new fans.

"I think if he gives it a little time and moves away from the show, because that can hold you back a bit or at least it can make people judge you in an unfavourable way, then he can do it. When I left *The X Factor* that's what I did. I went out in the second week of live shows so I was never going to have the same pressure or demands on me as someone who was in the show a lot longer but I do think it's helped me. I tried to get away from all that *X Factor* bandwagon because it can be a bit cheesy. I worked with a new artist called DJ Ironik and his song went to number five in the charts.

"Michael Jackson's producers heard a song I had recorded about my son and they liked it so they called up and asked me to come in and they were looking at that for his new album but then we lost Michael. It was still a great honour though.

"I'm working with Miss Frank from series six of *The X Factor* who are really cool and have a great sound together. Funnily enough, I've started to get lots of *X Factor* people come my way for help writing and producing their albums and it's good to work with them and take them in a new direction.

"I just think you see *The X Factor* as a great opportunity to meet all these people in the music industry and get your music out there to people who won't have heard of you before.

"Once you leave the show, I think you have to really get your head down and focus on your music rather than relying on the programme to do that for you. I think that gives you more confidence and if you do get dropped from a label, you'll have a bit more experience and know-how and perhaps it wouldn't be such a blow.

"I think Leon can do it though. He has everything going for him and there's no reason why he can't pull it back."

Niki Evans came fourth in the fourth series of *The X Factor* and has been busy performing in the West End in *Blood Brothers* and in pantomime since leaving the programme. She thinks that Leon wasn't prepared for the strains of the industry and that it was too much too soon for him. "Leon wasn't ready for the pressure of the music business," says Niki. "It's hard to keep picking yourself back up and starting again but in the future who knows?"

For others, though, the way Leon was marketed did him no favours. The shy singer who is incredibly humble and comes across as unsure of their talent might work well on TV but a more self-assured performer is likelier to do better in the charts.

"Leon Jackson was presented as the kind of under-confident performer model that's often wheeled out on *The X Factor*," says Fraser McAlpine. "He may be under-confident, he may love his mum a lot, he may cry a lot and those all might be things you do when you're on a TV programme like *The X Factor* and you might say those things and act that way and it might be genuine, but after a couple of weeks it doesn't really work. If you're in the final and then you win *The X Factor* then you'd think that he'd gain in confidence.

"When he released singles and his albums, he was still the same under-confident performer seen on *The X Factor* and people generally want pop stars to be vibrant and unusual. If being a singer is what you want most in the whole world then you act like it is when you win *The X Factor* and get in the charts. By carrying on with the template, it seemed really unfashionable and out of touch. Pop stars have to feel a breed apart."

Instead of being injected with a hit of bravado to boost his performances and apparently modest outlook, Leon Jackson acted coy when he was competing on the show. This might have been some of his charm for fans; that he didn't realise that actually he could hold a note or two and wasn't too bad at the singing lark. Needless to say, for Fraser this sheepish behaviour didn't help Leon when he took on the charts in his own bashful way.

"The way it was played out, it was like we were left hanging on waiting for the day Leon Jackson became more confident in his role," said Fraser. "Pop fans don't have that time, nor should they, and the industry doesn't work in that manner. Sure people develop over time but you can't magically give someone a performer's personality and make them more animated.

"There are other singers who actually have the performer personality, like Robbie Williams, like Mika, who entertain and give fans what they want. They put on a show, they seek to make their performances fun and give people a good time. They're the people who make brilliant pop stars and singers. They might not have the best voices and sometimes their music may not be the best but they can act up to the role.

"To be a great pop star you need to have an element of this because a lot of music is escapism and entertaining, especially if you don't have a voice that is out of the ordinary and don't have music that is distinct.

"Leona Lewis doesn't really have this performer element to her character but what she lacks in that she makes up for in talent. Leon didn't have a voice that was freakishly good and he didn't have songs that were that great and without this performer personality, he just completely faded into the background.

"He was still under-confident or at least was portrayed in that way and had nothing else really to rest his laurels on. That could have been because he was young and hadn't much experience but he just didn't seem to have all the components necessary to become a success in the charts and with music fans."

Unlike in days gone by, in the 21st century the ascent of a pop star must be short and painless. Sure, it's good to see how an artist has developed but reality/talent TV show winners need to make an impact in timely fashion and when they do, create a big splash as opposed to cautiously dipping their toe into the pool of pop.

"Waiting for someone to blossom just isn't viable in the charts because even if Leon Jackson does do it, by that point people have jumped on another bandwagon and that bandwagon is either the person who came runner-up to them or the new throng of contestants from the show," says Fraser. "But besides that, you can't base your career on being that under-confident a performer. Your fans can't hold your hands and reassure you all the way because unless you're doing something spectacular, there will be other people doing what you want to do better than you.

"That could have just been the way he was portrayed on TV and afterwards and the fact that Leon Jackson had little music experience beforehand but it just didn't work in the charts. He wasn't charismatic and he didn't have the music to cover any cracks in his lack of performer personality."

And while we're on the subject Fraser reckons that being a bit humble, shuffling around and looking at your shoes, is no way for a pop star to act. We are a country that has produced extrovert singers like Mick Jagger, Rod Stewart and Ozzy Osbourne, rock stars who dance like sex-obsessed robots, chuck microphone stands around like drum majors and, in the case of Ozzy, even bite the heads off bats. Surely we want a little more from our chart stars than the coy cock of the head and a modest shrug of the shoulders when informed they have a number one single.

"Being under-confident can't be the only thing to mark you out besides winning *The X Factor*," says Fraser. "If the music doesn't cut it and speak for you and your career is just based around you being under-confident and not really knowing what you're doing, it doesn't bode well. It just doesn't work well on stage because people want to be entertained and it doesn't work in pop in general because being a pop star should be the greatest job in the world and being coy and indifferent about it doesn't really wash. Replacing the *X Factor* tag with that of being under-confident, it's not really a great recipe for success."

Evidently not. Head of press for HMV Gennaro Castaldo has a different opinion on Leon's career post *X Factor*. Rather than Leon being unconfident as such, it's more that he's at a disadvantage in being a male solo singer at a time when the demand for male singers was pretty poor.

"The market for male solo singers is at a low at the moment," says Gennaro. "This could change but people don't seem to be buying it as much as they used to and even if they do, it's by the tried and tested performers: Robbie Williams, Will Young, James Morrison, Mika. There's not as much let-up for a new male singer, especially one singing ballads because even that isn't as popular as it was about 10 years ago.

"This can all change in the charts. It's all just a matter of what's popular at that moment in time and no one can really ever predict that but at the moment I think it's much harder for male singers to get picked up and become big because people are more interested in R&B, female singers and bands.

"It's unlucky for them and for Leon and all the other male winners to come from these programmes because they're at a disadvantage to begin with. The way the programmes are geared up is to find the latest new talent, so even if the market for male singers gets better, they might have missed the boat. A while back it was all Westlife and boy bands so it could revert back to that and Leon could find that he is in demand again but I think people tend to plump for the biggest performers in that genre, the Take Thats of this world."

While Take That might not be shaking in their boy band boots yet, Gennaro thinks that part of the trouble with Leon Jackson's image was that he was sold as a rather sophisticated jazzy singer on the programme but when he came out of *The X Factor* as a recording artist, and the nation's winner, the type of music he performed didn't match up to what was presented on the show, perhaps leaving some fans disappointed.

"I think also with Leon, and the same can be said of Steve Brookstein, the reason it didn't go as big as everyone expected was because he was on TV singing jazzy songs on TV and tapped into that Michael Bublé sound and then afterwards he didn't really seem to match up with the Leon Jackson people had seen on TV," says Gennaro. "Fans might have liked that version and theoretically could have voted for him because they liked that type of music. They might not have, but I don't think it helped to market him. But that's something that the singer has to help with as well. So from a fans' point of view, it's not consistent and it might have been hard for them to stay interested in his career.

"With Alexandra Burke, she was always an R&B singer and that's what she is in the charts, so it's a much more defined career path and means that any fans of her music from her *X Factor* days hopefully won't be disappointed with the direction she's gone in. She's always been an R&B singer so it makes sense for her to do that nowadays. It's the same for JLS who are now incredibly successful and for Leona Lewis who has had international success; they have gone on to record the type of music they sang in *The X Factor*.

"In fact, I think with all of the success stories on the programme, they've had a very clear idea of what type of artist they are from the start, which helps to market them in the show and afterwards, and create a fan base of people who like that genre and who will hopefully then go on to buy their music afterwards."

Too right. For Tony Lundon from Liberty X it is a combination of these things – the pressure of getting songs out, the pressure of deciding which songs to record and which direction to go in – that can lead to the winner being dropped from a label sooner than expected.

Tony thinks that for winners like Leon Jackson and Steve Brookstein, the nature of the programme means that they only have a short period of time as a priority for both the labels and the public, and that if they haven't enjoyed the success expected of them, if things aren't going so swimmingly for both the label and the singer, then the act can be out on its ear pretty quick to make room for the next winner waiting in the wings.

"I suspect that somewhere along the line, their labels decided they weren't a priority, or had no faith in them to begin with," says Tony. "Things can turn sour with labels for a multitude of reasons. Maybe they were at loggerheads with the powers-that-be over 'musical direction'. Maybe they refused to prostitute themselves 'artistically' or promotionally to the extent that the label demanded. Maybe their egos got the better of them.

"Maybe a member of the label team's ego got the better of them, or maybe they didn't have a decent manager to grease the political wheels, or they had one who was too busy trying to take 20% from so many different acts, there was no time to work any one of them properly."

And if the singer and the label are at odds with each other over the direction to take the music, or if the whippersnappers from the next year's show are coming through, then chances are the old winner will get pushed to one side. If that happens and the attention for the winner dips, then Tony reckons it's only a matter of time before fans, critics and the press see that you've been sidelined and turn their focus on the young bucks rising through the latest series' ranks.

"It was probably a combination of all of the above," says Tony. "When it comes to reality talent, as soon as the artist and their label pull in different directions, the artist is on a countdown. The label is already looking at the next 'priority', and when that filters through to the industry and the media, you're done."

Being done with might not sound like such a great position but Daniel DeBourg was glad to be free of the competition and the expectations the TV programme inadvertently placed upon contestants' heads. He thinks that contestants are often fighting a losing battle with their labels, and that to be free of that means they can get on with things rather than worrying about whether their single clashes with another contestant's release.

"I have total respect for Simon Cowell," says Daniel. "Forget about all this Mr Nasty Guy stuff, he's nice. He's a nice guy and he does know what he's talking about. Louis Walsh is great as well and you respect the time that the judges take working on you while you're on the programme because it is helpful and you respect their opinions and thoughts. I still think that now.

"I didn't like the songs I was given but it doesn't mean that you have to sing those songs for the rest of your life. It's just a TV programme when it comes down to it and while it may be a good TV programme that a lot of people like and get a lot from, you can't expect it to do everything for you

"I'm under a silence agreement for 14 years and it's the same for all the contestants on *The X Factor*. That's one of the reasons I'm glad I'm not associated with *The X Factor* nowadays and having that *X Factor* career because I have control over mine and I don't have to rely on the programme to make a name for myself.

"I don't feel I have to compete with everyone coming out of the show, because I'm behind the scenes doing things on my own terms. But for those who were in the show longer than me, they'll be signed to the same label and will be all going after the same market and releasing singles around the same time as each other. I think it's harder for acts who go that way afterwards.

"It's not their fault because it is a great opportunity and it's not really the label's fault because they have so many people to deal with but equally the label can't give priority to everyone, especially those who finished lower down or those who aren't getting the sales they thought they might. So often those contestants who finished further down in the show but are still signed with the label won't release music for a while and by the time they do release music, people might have forgotten about them.

"I think if you do have an idea of how you want your career to go it's almost better to just do it your own way and get on with it on your own terms. It's worked out well for me. I'd never look down on someone for doing it the other way but I think if you just bite the bullet, you get more of a reward. You get more of a steer on things and the success you have will be on merit and not just because of the programme."

Brother and sister duo Sarah and Sean Smith, aka Same Difference, were runners-up in the year that Leon Jackson won *The X Factor.* Since leaving the show, Sarah and Sean have toured and seen their debut album, *Pop*, reach gold status. They had an amicable parting with the label they were originally signed to on leaving *The X Factor,* Syco, and have since signed to PopLife.

Sarah Smith thinks that coming third in the contest left her and her brother with fewer expectations placed on them than might have been the case if they'd scooped the title, especially since as a pop act at a time when the pop market has dipped, they might not have had as much success as people might have expected, which in turn could have had them written off.

"It would have been brilliant to win *The X Factor* but we were chuffed with third place," says Sarah. "There wasn't the expectation laid on us to succeed when we came out. We are a pop act and we came out when pop wasn't really that strong and there wasn't really that much in the industry for pop music. I think if we had come out and won it, we would have been absolutely slated. Coming out third we wanted to better ourselves all along. We were like, 'OK we didn't win but how can we make ourselves better? What can we improve?'

"If we'd have been first we would have been slated by the media and the people who didn't vote for us. But I think people went, 'Oh you know what I actually like those guys' and they've kind of given us more of a chance."

As such Same Difference have flourished under their new management and are working on some new material. Both Sarah and

Sean had been performing for years, Sarah at drama school and Sean on a cruise ship, and were used to the auditioning process. Sarah thinks that *The X Factor* might have been daunting for Leon because he'd never been to an audition before appearing before those judges on the show and as such might not have been dealt the blows that come with being a performer.

"Personally, I think the thing with Leon was that *The X Factor* was his first ever audition," said Sarah. "He is a natural talent but because he hadn't really gone through auditions and gigs beforehand, he hadn't really had any knock-backs, which help you deal with things easier.

"I think it was all a bit mad and crazy for him and he probably thought, 'I didn't realise that this is what it's like'. I think that was why he struggled a bit more because he didn't understand the industry as much as he does now and so he didn't know how to play it."

Leon's inexperience aside, Sarah thinks that her pal had a hard time chart-wise after so much was made of Peter Kay's *X Factor* send-up 'The Winner's Song'. Kay turned himself into the portly character Geraldine McQueen, a contestant on his mock TV show *Peter Kay's Britain's Got The Pop Factor And Possibly A New Celebrity Jesus Christ Superstar Strictly On Ice* and, as Geraldine, released 'The Winner's Song' at the same time Leon released 'Don't Call This Love', which was written by Gary Barlow.

In the event, both Geraldine and Leon missed out on the top spot when pop singer Pink went to number one, leaving Geraldine at number two and Leon number three. "When Leon came out there was that chart battle with Peter Kay's song as Geraldine, which was just quite unfair on him," says Sarah. "Some people like to be down on *The X Factor* like they were with Joe McElderry in series six of *The X Factor*, and stopped the single from going to number one. People like to rebel against *The X Factor* and I think maybe that's part of the reason why his single wasn't quite as big as it should have been."

Maybe Leon can take comfort from the thought that his song and talents didn't seem to be an element in that particular chart race, more that it was a political step to prevent *The X Factor* and those involved with it pinching the top spot again. Once he is apart from the programme, he might stand more of a chance of getting on in the charts.

"Leon is a fantastic talent who has a lot more to give," says Sarah. "I think over the next couple of years he'll come back with something much bigger. Now he knows what the industry's all about and he's been in it for a couple of years, he'll come back fighting stronger."

Part of the problem with trying to turn a pound note for *X Factor* winners is that while they might achieve a certain level of success, if it isn't substantial enough then it's over quickly. "It is definitely a shame to cast someone off so early in their career but it is a very difficult business," says Sarah. "It either goes absolutely massive or it goes big but not big enough and the record labels are so used to having Westlife, Leona Lewis, Susan Boyle – massive success, absolutely huge artists.

"If you look at an act like Girls Can't Catch. They had a first single out that didn't do so well but now their second single is out and they're having a second push at it. If they were on Syco, Simon Cowell's record label, then that would be it if the second didn't do well so it's a catch-22 situation.

"When you're with *The X Factor* you have that massive exposure and you sell more copies because everyone knows about you but then people expect you to do better so there's a massive build-up to your release. But then at the same time you are on a label that has a higher expectation. It's crazy!"

Despite this, Sarah has had a positive experience with Syco and *The X Factor* in general and has experienced none of the negativity that people often associate with the label or big labels in general; not having any control or being pushed to one side. "We were definitely well supported by Syco," says Sarah. "There's a lot said about *The X Factor* and Syco being ruthless but we haven't experienced that. If you are nice to them, they are nice to you. We haven't had any trouble with them at all, they've been absolutely lovely."

Sarah remains level-headed about the change of record label and is content with her career; after all, she is getting to do what she's always wanted to do and she's getting paid for it. "The decision to part company was a business one," she says. "It wasn't, 'We hate Same Difference, we're going to drop them,' it was just that it hasn't sold as many as it could, we're going to make a loss if we carry on so it would be better to part on good terms, which we did.

"And now we're with PopLife and they're willing to do that with us and take us to Europe and Syco have been lovely. They've given us the album and called to wish us every success in the world. They didn't have to do that. It's lovely because you hear so many horror stories but we haven't had that at all.

"I think with this label, PopLife, they really love pop and they understand pop music because it's what they do. They have less expectation of us because they know more about the pop industry instead of the music industry as a whole. I think it's really going to help us because we're a really intimate act.

"I think you have to understand us because it's not every day you get a brother and sister singing cheesy pop. They either say, 'I don't get this at all, I don't know how to market that', or they go, 'I get it. This is like the music we had in the Nineties and we're going to bring it back'. You have people on both sides. But I think this time they know what me and Sean are all about."

Sarah's brother Sean is similarly pragmatic about his time on the show and career afterwards. Unlike some contestants who loathe the label they are assigned to on the show, he is chuffed that he and Sarah were given distinct identities, which helped to make them memorable during their time on the box. "I definitely think being branded during the show can help afterwards," he says. "The people you cling on to most are the people who are different. In series six of *The X Factor* Jedward popped out because they couldn't sing and then people slated them and you remember them. I remember Olly Murs from that series because I think of him as a cheeky chappie like Robbie Williams. We were given a niche that fitted us.

"At that time we were really happy to be there and we were really excited. The songs that were given to us leant themselves to that thing. We had massive crowds afterwards. Merchandising and gimmicks are a big thing for us. We're an act you can do that with so we were really lucky with the image they gave us.

"I think it didn't help us so much when we came out because we had to go to the outside world where we were hard to market. We were trying to do what *High School Musical* were doing but didn't have the movie to put the songs on the back of. We were given this sort of cheesy pop and people had a chance to love us or hate us, but it put us in good stead. Since we've been out, we've been doing gigs, we've been kept really busy.

"Even so, the biggest hype for us was on the show and nothing's going to top that. Even if our album does really well or is played all the time on the radio, it's still not as big as *The X Factor* because there you're singing to 15m people each week. But I have no regrets whatsoever. It's been great. We were handed our first album, which was written in a week, but with this one we've had longer and I think it's going to be a fun year. We've now got a couple of houses and all these things we would never have if we didn't have *The X Factor*."

For celebrity writer Mr Holy Moly, Leon Jackson was never going to cut it in the charts or in the world of celebrity because he was never sparkling enough, especially compared with runner-up Rhydian Roberts, and his voice wasn't as strong as other winners'.

"The really good celebrities are always good celebrities because they're good at something else. If you're looking at someone like Lindsay Lohan she's on magazines and is famous for being wasted. That's her career. But then you look at Lady Gaga or Tom Cruise who became celebrities because they're unique and celebrity is just the tittle-tattle that comes with their jobs.

"You can do that in reality TV. You can even argue that someone like Rhydian Roberts has done that. He is a good singer and walked out of the competition, didn't win it because everyone thought he was a joke at first but has done well.

"Then you look at Leon Jackson. He won but he was massively

boring. He answered a question no one was asking. No one is waiting with baited breath to find out what Leon Jackson is doing. People watch you on a TV show and that's pretty much it. Especially if you're boring and don't have really good songs to keep people interested."

So if you haven't got the songs and want to stay in the public eye then at least make sure you do something memorable like grow your fingernails really long and use them as a walking cane or renounce rock'n'roll after a sign from God.

# Chapter 10

# *The X Factor*
# Series Five & Six

Two more series, two more winners. Besides irking Leonard Cohen fans with her cover of 'Hallelujah', Alexandra Burke from the fifth series has gone on to pastures new and exciting since winning the series in 2008. Rapper 50 Cent – or Fiddy to pals – rated her work, fashion brand Dolce & Gabbana asked her to be the face of a new line and she's working on releasing her debut alum in the states.

"Alexandra has done really well over in the UK but they're having trouble marketing her in the US because even though 'Bad Boys' has Flo Rida on it, they still think it's too pop," says series four contestant Daniel DeBourg.

Only time will tell if her career will be as big as Leona's, Will's or Girls Aloud's have been. But the hangover of Leona's humungous success means that the people behind Alexandra seem to be taking more time and favouring letting Alexandra polish her sound instead of rush releasing something that isn't quite right.

"I have a CD of Alexandra Burke's single to review," says Fraser McAlpine. "On the blurb, they have made such a big deal of her not being like Leona and not being the next Leona. It's almost as if they want to keep them both completely distinct. Leona sings ballads, Alexandra does more upbeat stuff.

"The good thing about both of them is that their songs suit their voices, are current and appear to have had more time spent on them. You'd think that this combination would be good foundations for a pop career."

"The thing that marks Leona and Alexandra out is that they have international appeal and that helps sustain your career," says HMV's Gennaro Castaldo. "That beside, they have well-thought-out songs, great voices, were marketed in a clear way on the show and appeal to their fans."

Alexandra's successor, Joe McElderry, was a cute teen from South Shields. Though his first single didn't reach the top spot – due in part to a campaign to prevent *The X Factor* winner's single getting to number one and instead get Rage Against The Machine's 'Killing In The Name' to the top spot – Gennaro thinks that he'll be in a good position to have a fair crack at being a pop star when he brings out his first album.

"What they've done with Joe McElderry is smart because he's a lad who appeals to the pre-teen and teen market so they've made his first single quite Disney-ish," says Gennaro. "They've made it so that his run from the show to the charts is continuous and there was no attempt to go outside of the persona they've created for him as the cutesy boy with the big voice so he may prove to be very successful."

That he might. All together now, didn't they do well.

# Chapter 11

# Have Reality TV Shows Changed Music For The Better Or Worse?

Populist, brash, damaging. TV searches for new talent have been called all these things and worse over the past decade and yet they still attract massive audiences and fans year in year out. By their very nature, they're divisive. Drama ensues on the remaining big talent search *The X Factor* and many observers, including ex-contestant Tabby Callaghan, say that the music is only a fraction of what the programme is about.

Established acts like Radiohead, Sting, Elton John, newcomers La Roux and Calvin Harris have all criticised elements of the programmes in their time. And love them or loathe them, the programmes have changed the way in which we view celebrity. But they've also provided hours of entertaining TV as is expected from light entertainment shows.

"I think these talent shows have made it easy to be a celebrity," says gossip writer Mr Holy Moly, the anonymous front of house of holymoly.co.uk. "It's created the illusion that being a celebrity is easy and I think that it's changed the way we class celebrities because there are about 10 times more of them than there were five years ago.

"I think it's a lot harder now for any of the people coming out of these shows to have any sort of longevity because there are so many people who can always do it cheaper, more quickly and brashly and who are willing to sell themselves to be a celebrity nowadays, so they have that to compete with. There is a chance for people to have longevity when they're on the show but mainly for people who give the impression that celebrity is something that comes from being good at something and isn't the end aim."

Because of the changes in the way the public conceive celebrity, Mr Holy Moly believes that the high turnover of contestants and series means that we're only really there for the ride while it's on TV but once the hopefuls start trying to have pop careers, we lose interest. It has changed our and their expectations of a career afterwards. We think it will be short and, as such, the contestants know they have a limited period of time to hit the spot with us.

"*The X Factor* and the contestants they get nowadays are much more interesting than they were in the beginning," said Mr Holy Moly. "Twenty million were watching *The X Factor* last year at one point. Everyone loves the drama of the competition and no one gives a shit afterwards. The TV show is constantly there to get people talking, the format is inescapable and it creates talk.

"Then there's a period of two months after it's finished when the contestants are out at arena tours and recording or whatever and then people forget about it because by that time, something else is on. No one is waiting with baited breath to find out what Leon Jackson is doing. People watch you on a TV show and that's pretty much it. They don't expect much of the contestants afterwards and the contestants have wised up to it. They know they only have a few months to cash in on their fame before people stop caring."

So, the TV talent shows have changed our views on the types of careers contestants, winners or otherwise, realistically go on to have after the cameras have stopped rolling. The shows have resulted in singles sales from time to time but the reliance on fads – that is, the contestants themselves – is pretty hairy, says Q magazine editor Paul Rees. "They have increased sales of singles in some respects," he says. "In many respects, though, they amount to a monopoly and monopolies are always dangerous in my experience – especially ones that suggest short-term-ism and appealing to the lowest common denominator are good things."

Even if TV talent programmes have changed music for the worse, the upshot is that other musicians will be working harder to get their tracks recognised as an antidote to it all. "By nature it needs to become increasingly quick and confrontational – to reinvent itself, ramp up the shock factor over and over again," says Rees. "I hope more than suspect that there will be a profound reaction against this, since one extreme invariably leads to another, and we will see audiences clamouring for things of greater substance and depth."

Despite the list of winners who haven't done as well as expected there are those bright golden hopes – the Will Youngs, Girls Alouds and Leona Lewises – who've gone on to have solid music careers that are sturdier and more interesting than their peers who were discovered the 'hard way'.

They've created opportunities for existing acts to perform on the shows or mentor contestants at a time where mainstream music programmes do not exist. While some may moan about the shows monopolising the Christmas chart, others think it has made it more exciting.

"*The X Factor* has created an awful lot of money for record companies and for artists themselves," says HMV's Gennaro Castaldo. "It has also created a platform to launch talent and to bring the artist closer to the fans and vice versa. In the absence of a BBC pop music show, it has created opportunities for established successful pop artists to come on and promote their songs week after week.

"As we've seen from the Rage Against The Machine Facebook campaign, it can have a polarising effect on audiences but then 15 million people still watch it every year so on reflection, I'd say it is a very good example of what is popular and a representation of the mainstream charts and what works there.

"Others may feel that it has taken away the unpredictability of the charts but artists don't bother with the Christmas charts. People like Take That who are hugely successful, write great pop songs and have loyal fans, could have a really good stab at a Christmas single and probably get it to number one without too much effort but the fact is that artists don't bother. Either because they end up getting beaten by a novelty act, like Westlife did a few years back with Bob The Builder, and they got a bit of ribbing about that, which was quite embarrassing for them, or they concentrate on their album because album sales are everything nowadays. Singles don't really mean anything anymore. They are merely songs on an album and people can download whichever song they like from an album so in a way, they decide their singles.

"People look back on the Christmas number one with a real sense of misplaced nostalgia because in the past decade all we've had are later-stage Spice Girls, Bob the Builder, Mr Blobby.

"*The X Factor* at least puts a little effort in it and it's fair game. They get to number one so often at Christmas because people like the song and buy it. But I can see that people get frustrated by the impotence of it and the omnipresence of it.

"Whatever anyone says, *The X Factor* does have a function and it has filled a slot that was already there. *Top Of The Pops* has gone, and in its later stages it was dross. When I used to watch it as a kid it had proper rock and pop stars on it. It kind of lost meaning and was no longer valid.

"That said, for a kid of this generation, they might have thought it was brilliant. But now there's no weekly pop show, nothing on the BBC or Channel 4. People still want to watch music and that's what *The X Factor* does and that's why 15 million people watch it.

"The problem with reality TV shows that launch pop stars is by their very nature they have a quick turnover. This year's winner will soon be bringing out an album that four months later will be competing with the next winner of the show.

"They have to stand out and make sure their fans carry on from the show into the real world because they're up against all the people they were on the show with, plus all the established ones from previous series, the current crop and they have the added pressure of people saying, 'Oh look, that winner from last year isn't doing so well, you'll be there in a year'."

As we've seen, that is a very real possibility. But as many contestants have said, a shot at glory and a few jeers if it doesn't go as expected is better than not giving it all a shot.

"I'm very grateful to Simon for his show as it got me singing again and I've done a lot of things I've only dreamed about," says ex-contestant Niki Evans. "But it can be soul destroying on the other hand. *The X Factor* doesn't give you the fame and fortune. It only gives you a taste of it and then the work starts to find out who you are and what you're going to do.

"So you have to remember not to take it too seriously. It's a great ride while it lasts so you have fun and enjoy it because there will be a lot of hard work to come for the majority whose *X Factor* dreams will never come true."

Exactly. These shows are competitions. The contestants go on the journeys they tell us about in their talking heads. We get riled by contestants who get too bolshy or who are vanilla. We want the underdogs to win. We get irritated by releasing covers of songs that we don't feel needed covering. We get wound up by their dodgy makeovers and by het-up judges. We cry or shout at the telly when they win.

We support their endless list of charitable causes for which they contribute on group singles. We forget about them when someone else with a slightly different voice comes along and does the very same thing the year after. But we wouldn't have it any other way. As Tony Lundon says, "God is it entertaining." And that is why we'll probably keep on watching, voting and investing our time – even for a short time – in these singers for years to come. And the singers themselves who wise up to it all will push out singles quickly to appeal to us while we're interested. What will happen next year? Probably the same as the year before and the year before that. But would we miss it for the world? No. Happy viewing.